CREATIVE HOMEOWNER®

THE SMART APPROACH TO DESIGN:
BATHROOMS
REVISED AND UPDATED 3RD EDITION

THE SMART APPROACH TO DESIGN:
BATHROOMS
REVISED AND UPDATED 3RD EDITION

Complete Design Ideas to Modernize Your Bathroom

Editors of Creative Homeowner,
and Tech Editor Kristina McGuirk

CRE▲TIVE HOMEOWNER®

The Smart Approach to Design: Bathrooms

Printed in China

Current Printing (last digit)
10 9 8 7 6 5 4 3 2 1

ISBN 978-1-58011-573-5

Library of Congress Cataloging-in-Publication Data

Names: Creative Homeowner Press.
Title: The smart approach to design bathrooms.
Other titles: Bathrooms
Description: Updated edition. | [Mount Joy, PA] : Creative Homeowner, [2023]
 | Previous editions published 2011 and 2018. | Includes index.
Identifiers: LCCN 2018000103 | ISBN 9781580118040
Subjects: LCSH: Bathrooms--Remodeling. | Bathrooms--Design and construction.
Classification: LCC TH4816.3.B37 S625 2018 | DDC 690/.42--dc23
LC record available at https://lccn.loc.gov/2018000103

We are always looking for talented authors. To submit an idea, please send a brief inquiry to acquisitions@foxchapelpublishing.com.

Creative Homeowner® is an imprint of New Design Originals Corporation and distributed exclusively in North America by Fox Chapel Publishing Company, Inc., 800-457-9112, 903 Square Street, Mount Joy, PA 17552.

Acknowledgments

The editors wish to thank designers Mallory Lunke and Plural Design Studio; Mel Bean Interiors; Mary Patton Design; the team at Golden Rule Builders; Helene Goodman, IIDA; Susan Obercian, of European Country Kitchens; and Lucianna Samu for their contributions to this book.

We would also like to acknowledge the helpful information provided by the National Kitchen and Bath Association, and the resources provided by representatives of the numerous brands who contributed to this book.

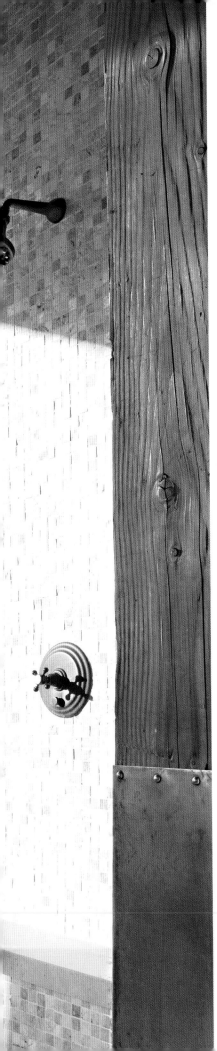

Contents

INTRODUCTION

Every room in your home has the potential to showcase your personal style, and your bathroom is no exception. Nowadays, bathrooms combine function with style, incorporating materials, surfaces, and textures that used to be confined to other areas of the home. In addition, there are many functional elements that bathrooms contain, including fixtures, fittings, cabinets, lighting, and ventilation systems.

The many options in fixtures, materials, and finishes that are available today allow you to create your own style in the bath.

The Smart Approach to Design: Bathrooms will
• explain all of these components,
• explain the features that will fit in best with your lifestyle and needs, and
• highlight stylish features you can make your own.

Want a modern sink, a Euro-style bathtub, or traditional fixtures? How about marble countertops, tile floors, or mirrored accents on the walls? Go for it—any style can be incorporated into your home to create a bathroom you will love for both the way it functions and its good looks.

Bathroom decor may run the gamut from ultra modern to classic, such as old world (above), or a combination of contemporary and nostalgic styles (right).

CHAPTER 1
THINKING AHEAD

It can be a good idea to remodel or add another bathroom, even in a tough economy. An updated design or a second bath will increase the value and livability of your house. The most important thing you can do prior to the start of your project is to prepare. Know what you need, what you'd love to have, and how you're going to pay for it. And find the best people to get the job done right. This is one of those remodeling projects that you'll never regret!

Thinking about adding a bath or remodeling an old one? Plan ahead to make the most of your time, money, and space.

Assessing Your Needs

At the outset, make a list of what you would like your new bathroom to be and how you need it to function. Will it be your at-home spa? A shared bath for the family? Simply a practical extra bath? The type of bathroom—and who will use it—may determine its size and will certainly affect the products you select to finish it.

If you're remodeling an existing bath, it's good to make a list of what you don't like about it and what you hope to change. Is there enough storage? Is the lighting around the vanity or lav suitable for grooming? Are the fixtures functioning efficiently? Is the ventilation adequate?

Maybe you'd like to replace your one-piece tub and shower with an extra-deep soaker and a walk-in rain shower. Perhaps the materials—tiles, vanity countertop, faucets, light fixtures, and so forth—should be updated.

Take safety measures into account in your analysis. Are there enough ground-fault circuit interrupters (GFCIs)? These receptacles should be installed in wet areas, such as bathrooms, because they can sense an imbalance in the electrical circuit and cut the current in a fraction of a second. Unlike GFCIs, ordinary receptacles cannot protect you against the full force of an electrical shock.

Other safety concerns about an older bath can be the condition of the floor tiles—are they cracked or slippery? How old are the faucets? Are they equipped with anti-scalding mechanisms?

Don't forget to take ergonomics into account, especially if older family members will use the room. Are the valves easy to open and close? Is it easy or difficult to enter the tub or shower? Are there grab bars?

TOP RIGHT: You can still live large in a modest size bath. Here, a mirrored wall visually enlarges the room and counterbalances the visual weight of the large, dark vanity.

RIGHT: Sliding screens reveal storage and a dressing room in an adjacent space.

FAR RIGHT: Overall, a neutral color scheme is calm and timeless.

Q&A

Can I replace a bathtub and small shower in my primary bath with just a large walk-in shower? I heard that this was a no-no.

what the experts say

Real estate and remodeling experts both say that a house without a bathtub will lower the resale value. Most people with young children who are buying a house want at least one bathtub. However, you're talking about the primary bath, and assuming there is another bathroom with a tub in your house, you're probably safe with just a shower, especially if it's large and has desirable spa features.

what real people do

Many people are forgoing a bathtub to make space for a large walk-in shower, especially when they are planning to stay in their house for at least five years. All the experts would agree that, in this case, the most important thing you can do is make your bath what you want it to be. For people who rarely, if ever, use the tub, a great shower makes a lot of sense.

In fact, when you put your house on the market, depending on who is buying, a glamorous custom shower for two with multiple showerheads and sprayers, steam, and other luxe features may even seal the deal.

A spa shower has some serious benefits, but a generous soaking tub may be more your speed. Looking for a style upgrade? Splurge on an elegant floor tile or sleek, trendy fixtures. It's your money, spend it on your priorities

Making a (Wish) List and Checking It Twice

Go ahead and make your wish list as long as you like. Remember: you're only wishing at this stage, so the sky's the limit. This is a good time to visit bath design showrooms and home centers and to jot down ideas that you may have seen online or on TV. When it's available, note the cost.

Go over your list, making sure that what you've got on it is both practical and affordable for your circumstances. Be sure to consider your lifestyle: a gorgeous, jetted tub may be some people's idea of luxe bathing. But if you're strictly a shower person, don't be afraid to forgo the tub and build a fabulous shower in its place.

When you come up with a close-to-perfect plan, look for areas to trim expenses in case your budget were to become an issue. Decide what you really can't live without. Then, determine areas where you can substitute or make compromises. For example, rather than selecting real stone, choose a ceramic tile that looks like stone, but is more affordable.

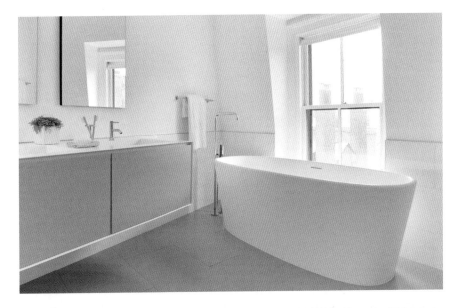

The simplicity of its style belies the exacting execution of all the features that make this primary bath so perfectly pampering.

FAR RIGHT: A frameless glass shower enclosure keeps the elegant Carrara marble subway tiles on view. A rain shower and a handheld sprayer offer versatility. For more indulgence, there is a large soaking tub in the room as well.

it's in the DETAILS

TOP RIGHT: A heated towel rack is conveniently located on the wall above the tub. The location of the property allows the windows to remain uncovered.

BOTTOM RIGHT: The room also features a pair of vanities. Although only one is pictured here, they are identical.

Plan to Save

Once you decide to remodel or add another bath to your house, you'll have to do some important research and planning. Becoming informed and knowing exactly what you want, how much you can or are willing to spend, and who is going to do the work will help you avoid some of the pitfalls that can cost you time and money.

Few people actually enjoy crunching numbers. However, establishing a budget is the only way to determine the size and scope of the project you can afford to design. It's disappointing to plan a luxurious bath, complete with spa features, only to find that you can barely afford a rain shower and a heated towel bar. Set priorities.

When you're looking at financing options, try to avoid paying cash. If it comes down to a choice between paying cash for remodeling or for buying a new car, always go the cash route for the car and finance the remodeling. You can deduct the interest of the home improvement loan from your taxes; you can't deduct the interest on a car loan. Unfortunately, many homeowners will gladly put money up front for a remodeling project and finance the car. It doesn't make sense.

It also doesn't make sense to set aside money or sign a loan for thousands of dollars without getting a handle on where that money is going. How much time would you spend investigating new cars before buying? You would probably read performance reports on various makes and models, then test drive several vehicles before finally making a purchase. Approach a home improvement loan the same way. Take the time to investigate your financing options and all of the products and services for which you will be paying.

And don't forget: when seeking estimates, comparison shop for contractors. Use the plans and specifications for your new bathroom to get equivalent bids. If you can't draw them yourself, pay an architect or designer to do it.

3 THINK GREEN

2 RESEARCH PRODUCTS

TOP 10
Planning Points

Going into the project with a clear, detailed picture will help a big project run smoothly.

1. Set realistic goals by considering both your space and budget. Get pricing for products, as well as labor. What are the costs? What's your budget? How long would you need to save to get the space you want?

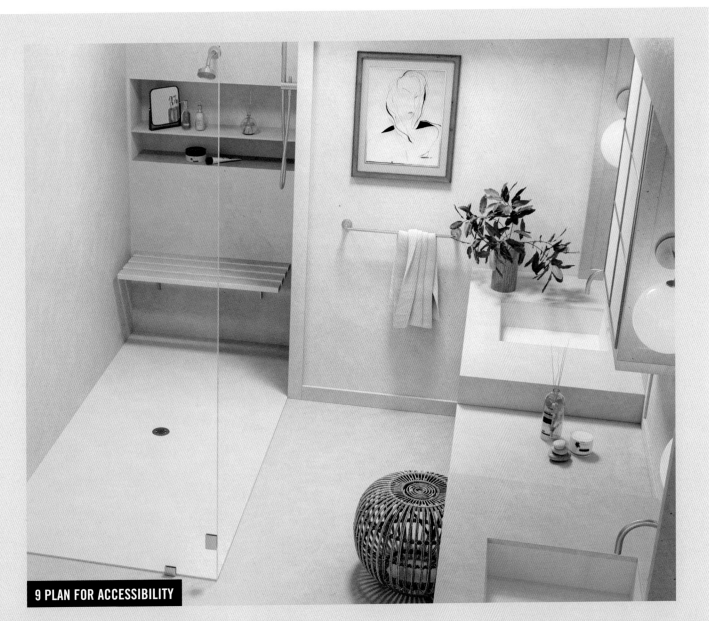

9 PLAN FOR ACCESSIBILITY

2. Research products to get yourself familiar with what's available today. Walking through home design centers or flipping through product lookbooks and catalogs can help tremendously.

3. Think green and identify ways to incorporate Earth-friendly products, such as water-conserving fixtures and sustainably or locally sourced materials. Reuse what you can, like painting an old vanity for new life.

4. Interview several professionals to find someone you'll feel comfortable and confident working with—whether that's a designer, architect, or contractor. Check their references and standing with the Better Business Bureau.

5. Assess your skills if you're considering doing some of the work yourself. Be honest. Can you really do it? Will the project be up to code?

6. Expect the unexpected. Be ready for project delays or budget increases due to labor, supply chain, or availability issues.

7. Make arrangements if the only bathroom in your house will be out of commission for a while during a renovation.

8. Obtain permits. Never let anyone tell you to skip this step. Permits and building codes exist for a reason—your safety. Ignoring them may cost you, not only financially, but personally, as well.

9. Plan for accessibility by including universal design principles and meeting ADA standards. These ideas are about creating spaces that are safe and usable for everyone, regardless of age or ability. Sometimes this is discussed as "aging in place."

10. Look beyond the layout for opportunities to build the bath of your dreams. Maybe a hallway linen closet can be used to house a steam generator, or a bedroom wall will come down for the ultimate primary suite.

A spacious floor plan that accommodates a double vanity, a large walk-in shower, and a separate soaking tub may require additional space. Expanding an existing home is a large and costly project. Most people will obtain a home improvement loan to get the job done. Interest on such loans is usually tax deductible, but consult your accountant.

FINANCING

Any bank or lending institution will tell you how much you can afford to spend on your home remodeling project. But if you feel more comfortable running a test on your own, here is a quick and simple overview of how banks figure out what you can spend.

THE DEBT-TO-INCOME (DTI) RATIO

This tells a lender if you can handle more debt on your current level of income. While each lender has its own approved DTI ratio, the average is normally at least 45 percent.

		EXAMPLE
*Current monthly expenses:	$ _____	$1,800
Add the estimated monthly remodeling payment:	+ $ _____	+ $200
Total expenses:	$ _____	$2,000
Divide by your gross monthly income:	÷ $ _____	÷ $5,000
This is your DTI ratio:	_____ %	.4 × 100 = 40%

*Credit reporting expenses—things like utilities and cell phone bills are not included.

HOW TO FIND YOUR MAXIMUM PAYMENT FOR REMODELING

If your DTI doesn't qualify for financing options, you may need to lower the monthly remodeling expenditure. This calculation will show you how low you need to go.

Gross monthly income:	$ _____	$5,000
Multiply by lender's DTI ratio:	× _____ %	× 45%
Subtotal:	$ _____	+ $2,250
Subtract your total monthly expenses (minus the estimated remodeling payment):	– $ _____	– $1,800
This gives you your maximum payment of:	$ _____	$450

*Still credit reporting debts only.

If the last line is negative, you may have to scale back your plans or do the work yourself on a very tight budget. A negative number means that you won't be receiving funds from a lender. However, you can check out other funding options. For example, a consolidation loan will allow you to incorporate your current debts into your home improvement loan. Firstly, this will lower the monthly cost of your current debts. Secondly, this loan allows you to deduct the interest from your taxes, something that you can't do on other forms of debt.

If your credit score is good, you can find a variety of other forms of financing as well. You could take out a loan against investments, borrow against your credit card, or the perennial favorite: obtain a private loan from a family member.

Seeking Help!

Ask friends and neighbors to recommend professionals in your area. You can also check online or in the local paper. Whenever you hire people to work in your home, first take the time to research them carefully. Your home is likely your largest single asset. Don't take chances with it unnecessarily. Interview professionals and follow up on their references. Ask tough questions. Call state agencies and trade associations to check credentials, and always work with licensed contractors.

Also remember, the people you hire to work on the project are in your home. You have every right to tell them not to smoke, play music, curse, or eat inside. You can even tell them how and where to store tools and materials around your home. Be reasonable, but make a set of rules before work begins, and ask your contractor to enforce them. You could include this in your contract, which gives you legal grounds for making your demands. However, in most cases, a reputable contractor will make sure that workers are respectful of your wishes.

Which brings us to the next question: should you do any of the job yourself? That depends on two things—your skills and whether or not a licensed professional is required by law. Take the quiz on the opposite page to see whether you've got what it takes; regarding the latter, check with your building department.

Assess your confidence in what projects you can do yourself. Perhaps you feel confident wallpapering and changing faucets or showerheads, but tiling or changing a light fixture isn't your thing. Find design and building professionals you can work with to make the project complete.

SHOULD YOU DO IT YOURSELF?

Before you make the decision to tackle a bath remodeling project on your own, take a few minutes to answer the following questions. This exercise will help you determine whether or not you have the necessary skills and abilities. Make sure to be honest with yourself.

YES	NO	Do you enjoy physical work?
YES	NO	Are you persistent and patient? (Do you have reliable work habits? Once the project is started, will it get finished?)
YES	NO	Do you have all the tools needed and, more importantly, the skills required to do the job?
YES	NO	Are your skills at the level of quality you need for this project?
YES	NO	Do you have time to complete the project? (Always double or triple the time estimated for a DIY project, unless you are highly skilled and familiar with that type of project.)
YES	NO	Will it matter if the project remains unfinished for a period of time?
YES	NO	Are you prepared to handle the kind of stress this project will create in your family relationships?
YES	NO	Have you done all of the steps involved in the project before?
YES	NO	Have you obtained the installation instructions from the manufacturers of the various products and fixtures to determine whether this is a project you still want to undertake? (You can obtain them from most manufacturers before purchase to determine the steps involved in installation and the skill level required.)
YES	NO	Is this a job that you can accomplish completely by yourself, or will you need assistance? If you'll need help, what skill level is involved for your assistant? If you need a professional subcontractor, do you have access to a skilled labor pool?
YES	NO	Are you familiar with local building codes and permit requirements? (Check into these matters before beginning work on your bathroom project.)
YES	NO	What will you do if something goes wrong and you can't handle it? (Most contractors are wary about taking on a botched DIY job, and many just won't. The liability is too high.)
YES	NO	Is it safe for you to do this project? (If you are unfamiliar with roofing for a bathroom addition, or do not have fall-protection restraints, you may not want to venture a roofing job. Similarly, if you know nothing about electricity, leave it to the professionals. Some jobs can have serious consequences if not performed correctly. Your health and safety should be the primary concerns.)
YES	NO	Can you obtain the materials you need? (Who will be your supplier?)
YES	NO	Are you attempting to do it yourself for financial reasons? (If so, have you looked at all your costs, including the cost of materials, your time, and the tools you need to purchase? If you are new to the DIY game, you may also want to consider the cost to correct any mistakes you may make. Will it still be a cost-saving venture given all of these factors?)
YES	NO	If you are trying DIY for your personal satisfaction, can you really guarantee a job will be done well? (If it doesn't come out right, how will you feel? Will you need the money to redo any unsatisfactory work? Will you have it? Will you be able to live with mistakes?)

SMART APPROACH: KNOW THE PROS

ARCHITECTS

If you're planning a significant structural change, such as expanding space or your bath will be part of a larger remodeling project, consulting an architect is a wise move. Among other things, an architect will be sensitive to making sure that the new bath blends with your home's original architecture. Be sure to find one who specializes in residential design. Look for the letters "AIA" after an architect's name. This indicates his or her membership in the American Institute of Architects, a national organization of licensed professionals. For a referral to an architect in your area, go to www.AIA.org.

CERTIFIED BATH DESIGNERS

Certified Bath Designers, or CBDs, are trained professionals who are certified specifically in bath design and remodeling by the National Kitchen and Bath Association (NKBA). Because CBDs are specialists, they can advise you with regard to spatial issues and floor plans, as well as offer you advice about the latest trends and innovations in bath products that would suit your needs and lifestyle. Check local bath-design showrooms or home centers to find a qualified professional with the letters "CBD" after their name. Or, log on to www.NKBA.org for a referral.

INTERIOR DESIGNERS

Interior designers don't make structural changes, but they work with color, pattern, texture, and furnishings to shape a design. You may want to contact an interior designer if you're interested in making significant aesthetic changes. The letters "ASID" after an interior designer's name indicate membership in the American Society of Interior Designers, a national organization of qualified licensed professionals. Check out www.asid.org to find a local or state chapter that can refer you to a member in your area.

CONTRACTORS

A contractor is a good choice if you have already hired an architect to design the bathroom or if you're not making substantial structural changes to the room. One good example of when to choose a remodeling contractor is when you're simply upgrading fixtures or reconfiguring the existing space for a better arrangement. Design-build remodeling firms offer one-stop shopping for design services and construction, with both designers and remodelers on staff. If something goes wrong, you only have to make one call.

ACCESSIBILITY AND AGING SPECIALISTS

Looking to make safety and accessibility a priority? Look for designers and builders with credentials that indicate they have relevant training—such as Certified Aging in Place Specialist (CAPS), Universal Design Certified Professional (UDCP), and Certified Living in Place Professional (CLIPP).

Q&A

Can you get out of a contract? What happens if something unforeseen happens that may affect going through with the project?

what the experts say

There is a grace period wherein you have the legal right to change your mind. This is called the "Right of Rescission." You can do this within three days of signing the contract without any liability if the contract was obtained at any place other than the designer's or contractor's office—your home, for instance. Federal law mandates that consumers must be made aware of this right in writing. Ask your contractor before you sign anything.

what real people do

Frank and Betty were excited about adding a primary bath to their 50-year-old house, but life happens. Just one week after signing a contract with a home improvement company, Frank had a health crisis that meant months of recuperation at home and additional strains on the couple's budget. Several days past the grace period, their legal right to cancel the job had expired—or did it?

Actually, Frank and Betty had never been properly informed of their right—the contractor failed to include it in the contract. By law, the Right of Rescission remains open beyond three days (up to three years) if the notice is not given or, as in Frank and Betty's case, is not provided in the required manner.

To ensure that you get what you want, put it in writing. If you like compact fixtures, such as the toilet and lav, specify the make and model numbers. Unless an item is custom, such as this vanity, provide manufacturer names, sizes, and colors in the contract.

The Write Stuff

You have a right to a specific and binding contract. The more specific details it contains, the better—the details will save you in the long run. Remember: anytime you enter into an agreement, you're venturing into the legal world of a litigious society. Get everything in writing, but know what you're signing—and never sign an incomplete contract.

For starters:

- Make sure the contract contains the contractor's name and proper business name as it appears on the business license, as well as the company's address, phone number, and business license number
- Details of everything the contractor will do, including such things as daily and final cleanup and security measures
- A complete list of materials and products, including size, color, model, and brand name of each one
- The approximate start and completion dates

GET SMART
ACCEPTING DELIVERIES

Let your contractor sign for deliveries unless you personally ordered the materials or are prepared to be liable for them. Signing for materials is your contractor's responsibility. Imagine what would happen if you signed for the wrong floor tiles. You would be responsible. Don't take chances. Let your contractor shoulder the burden of tracking down incomplete, incorrect, or damaged orders.

Special orders, such as this tub, can be tricky, and it's not uncommon for the wrong model to be delivered. Leave it to your contractor to handle these things.

What Else?

To prevent changes being made without your knowledge, your signature should be required on all plans before work begins. If you want to make a change during the course of the project, you'll probably need what is called a "change order." The procedure for handling changes should be spelled out in your contract and should require both your signature and the contractor's.

Don't hesitate to ask about any detail concerning the project. It's your house, and it's your money. The more information you have, the happier you will be with the result. This is particularly true when selecting products or figuring out warranty coverage. You can ask for a listing and full description of warranties that cover materials and workmanship—find out what is and isn't covered. Warranties are normally in force for one year and should be identified as either "full" or "limited."

Finally, it's wise to ask your contractor for waivers of lien, which release you from liabilities for subcontractors and manufacturers. At the end of the job, ask for a final lien waiver for each person who worked on the project to protect yourself from third-party debts and obligations. You don't want to be forced, legally, into paying for the job a second time because the contractor never made good on his debts.

All of the above should be part of the contract, along with anything else you feel should be spelled out clearly and in writing.

GET SMART WARRANTIES

Many manufacturers won't honor a warranty if an amateur fix-it job has been attempted. Avoid disasters by calling your contractor or the manufacturer for guidance about repairs.

Don't make changes if you don't have to, because they create additional work and delay progress. For example, substituting a wall-mounted faucet for one installed on the deck of a lav or vanity would entail opening and retiling a portion of the wall.

Insurance and Permits

All contractors should have current liability insurance and worker's compensation to cover employees while they are working on your property.

If you're still worried about your legal liabilities should an injury occur while someone is working on your property, talk to your insurance carrier and attorney. You may want your insurance agent to review the plans for the new bathroom and adjust your homeowner's coverage during the length of the project.

Never allow work to be done on your home without a legal permit. Permits may require fees and inspections—two things everyone would like to avoid—but they ensure the project conforms to the latest building codes.

A bathroom remodel requires hiring various workers. Tiling and plumbing call for different skills than installing new windows. Your contractor will hire qualified people and should be responsible for their on-the-job safety.

GET SMART
CHANGE ORDER

What if your contractor substitutes another product for the one specified in your written agreement? That is not cool, and you don't have to accept it. Tell him or her that you will only allow changes that have been properly outlined in writing and have both of your signatures. Any change order should include a detailed description of the work that will be involved and an estimate of the time and cost of making the change.

A bath can be your personal spa, but not if your contractor ignores your stated preferences.

Abundant natural light and natural materials emphasize this bathroom's Earth-friendly point of view.

FAR RIGHT: Because bathrooms are typically big water guzzlers, the homeowner and designer looked for water-efficient fixtures. In addition, the wall-mounted lav and toilet are ADA compliant, which means they conform to the standards outlined in the Americans with Disabilities Act.

it's in the DETAILS

TOP RIGHT: In one corner, a shower takes in sunlight, thanks to the glass enclosure, which is partially frosted for privacy.

BOTTOM RIGHT: The deep tub has the added convenience of a handheld sprayer for rinsing hair or bathing the family pet.

CHAPTER 2

SPACE PLANNING

How you arrange space is an important part of your new bathroom. In the previous chapter, you assessed your needs and made a wish list to inform things, like your budget. Now, it's time to use that list to think about the space you want to create, while also asking yourself how the bath will be used, when, and by how many people. Answering these questions is important to determining the best layout for the space.

Whether a task-oriented guest bath, a spa-like primary bath, or a busy bath for the whole family, smart planning can help you efficiently accommodate everything you need.

Take a look at the layouts and arrangements in this chapter. Then start thinking about what might work best for you.

Lay It Out

Whether it's a full-size bath or a powder room, the arrangement of space plays a large role in how well the room will function. This is as true for new builds as it is for remodels, but existing homes pose the added challenge of working with existing layouts.

A bathroom addition to an outside wall of the house offers the best possibilities for unencumbered floor space when renovating. However, it will be the costliest. One way to save money is to bump out the wall by a few feet and extend the existing floor structure out over the foundation. Consult an architect or builder first, to make sure the structure is sound and can carry the additional load. Always inquire about local zoning ordinances and setback requirements that may affect your plans before proceeding. If you violate codes, you could be forced to remove the new construction.

If an addition isn't an option, take a good look at what's next to the bathroom. Even a small amount of space stolen from a closet or an adjacent room can be the answer to your problem. Undeveloped areas like basements and attics may also be an option.

Some layouts separate bathing and toileting areas.

Additions are a great opportunity to create baths with a connection to the outdoors, like this luxurious walk-out steam-enhanced shower.

Floor-Plan Ideas

Bathroom layouts are as varied as any room in the home.
Check out the floor plans throughout this chapter to inspire your project.

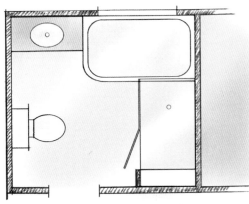

Large Tub and Walk-in Shower

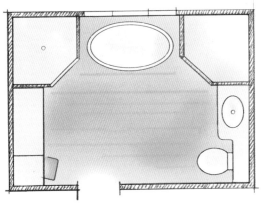

Shower Room and Freestanding Tub

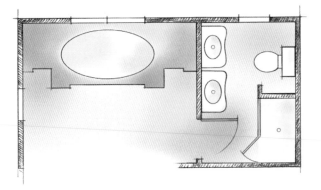

Separate Compartments

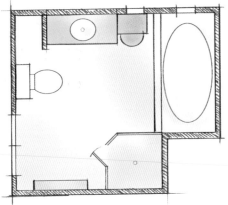

Platform Tub and Corner Shower

SMART APPROACH: PUT IT ON PAPER

Remodeling an existing bath? Take these steps to understand your space, which can help with replacing existing fixtures, estimating costs of new surface materials, and deciding if an alternate layout is an option.

MEASURE AND SKETCH

Begin by documenting the room as it now exists. Include adjacent areas that might be used for expansion. Start taking measurements, beginning with the length and width of the room. Then working from one corner, measure the location of all windows, doors, and walls. Record the swing of each door. Draw a rough sketch of the space with these measurements.

Measure and draw the cabinetry and plumbing fixtures, and indicate their heights. Measure the centerline of sinks, toilets, and bidets, and show how far the center of each of these fixtures is from the wall. Be sure to list the overall lengths and widths. Indicate light fixtures, outlets, and heat registers. Note load-bearing walls.

DRAW A FLOOR PLAN

For something a little more accurate, you can transfer your drawing and notes to graph paper with grids marked at 1/4-inch intervals. This formal drawing is called a "base map" or a "base plan." Draw it to a scale of 1/2 inch equal to 1 foot. Be as accurate as possible.

Refer to the base plan and your notes when you're creating a new layout for the space, which you will draw in the same manner. As you're plotting new fixtures, keep in mind that state and local codes may apply, especially to things like front and side clearances—even your existing space may not be up to current code. Ask about clearances when you apply for a permit if you're doing the actual work yourself. Of course, you can play it safe and consult a professional.

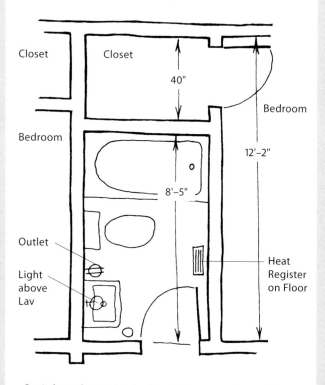

Begin by making a sketch of the bathroom as it now exists. Include any adjacent areas that might be used for expansion. Indicate fixtures and electrical and heating features.

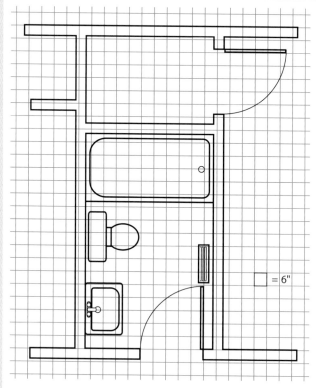

Use your rough sketch to create a base plan that is drawn to a scale of ½ inch to 1 foot. This time, be as accurate as possible when indicating measurements.

These homeowners created a main bath to fit their needs by combining a small bath with an adjacent powder room, also stealing an extra foot of space from a bedroom closet so they could meet code requirements. The archway is a functional and aesthetic choice—it masks the change in ceiling height between the two previously disconnected spaces. It also inspired other arched accents in the room (see more of this space in chapter 4).

1. BUILT-IN STORAGE

2. SLIDING DOORS

TOP 10
Best Uses of Space

1. **BUILT-IN STORAGE.** Use space inside the wall, between the stud, to create storage without impacting the floorspace.

2. **SLIDING DOORS.** Pocket doors slide into the wall, while barn-doors slide across the wall. Both save space by not swinging into a room.

9. PRIVACY GLASS

10. CORNER FIXTURES

3. MULTIPLE SHOWERHEADS. Installing a rain, handheld, and wall-mount showerhead offers multiple experiences in one shower and accommodates the needs of different users.

4. HALF WALLS. This is one way to create separate areas in a modest-size bath without closing it off to light sources in the room.

5. SKYLIGHTS. Installing one of these units allows you to have natural light where adding a standard window is not practical.

6. TUB/SHOWER COMBOS. These units are common for a reason: they maximize space and plumbing connections.

7. WATER CLOSETS. A closed-door compartment, just for the toilet, offers more privacy in a shared bath.

8. MEDICINE CABINETS. A medicine cabinet or two provides the expected mirror at the vanity while also adding storage.

9. PRIVACY GLASS. Whether on a water closet door or shower surround, frosted glass and other privacy glass allow light into the enclosed area while still offering some privacy.

10. CORNER FIXTURES. Showers, lavs, vanities, and toilets designed to tuck neatly into a corner are great solutions for small bathrooms or powder rooms.

Designing a Primary Bath

Compartmentalizing space makes sense when a bath is shared. Some of the best floor plans for today's primary or en suite baths include a compartment just for the toilet (water closet), and separate bathing and grooming areas. This concept makes lots of sense: it provides privacy and enough space for two people to comfortably use the bathroom at the same time.

Spa features are high on the list for most primary bathrooms, and they may include such amenities as a jetted or extra-deep soaking tub, a spacious walk-in shower equipped with steam or massaging water jets, or even access to the outdoors.

Don't forget to include plenty of storage space. Linens, grooming supplies, and cleaning products are common, but as part of a large suite, the bathroom may also connect to a walk-in closet or dressing area.

Other popular amenities for your consideration? A TV, fireplace, laundry, or coffee station. Sure, you have space and budget limitations, but don't stop yourself from exploring all the possibilities. This is where you start and end your day—go ahead and pamper yourself.

There's something quite luxurious about a walk-in shower or grand soaking tub bathed with natural light. Operable skylights also provide excellent ventilation when the weather is fair.

Primary Bath Design Options

Many primary baths are full baths, meaning they have a separate tub and shower, or combination tub and shower.

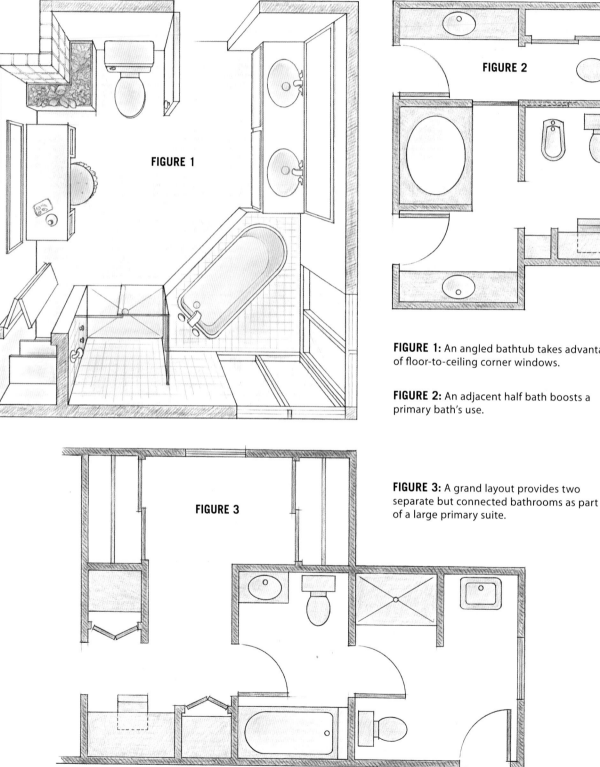

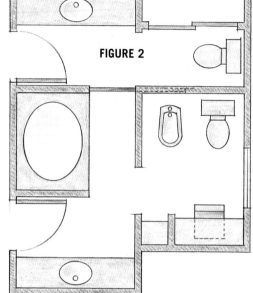

FIGURE 1: An angled bathtub takes advantage of floor-to-ceiling corner windows.

FIGURE 2: An adjacent half bath boosts a primary bath's use.

FIGURE 3: A grand layout provides two separate but connected bathrooms as part of a large primary suite.

Same idea, different spaces: Side by side but separate, a tub and shower occupy one end of a primary bathroom. This arrangement leaves space for a long double vanity.

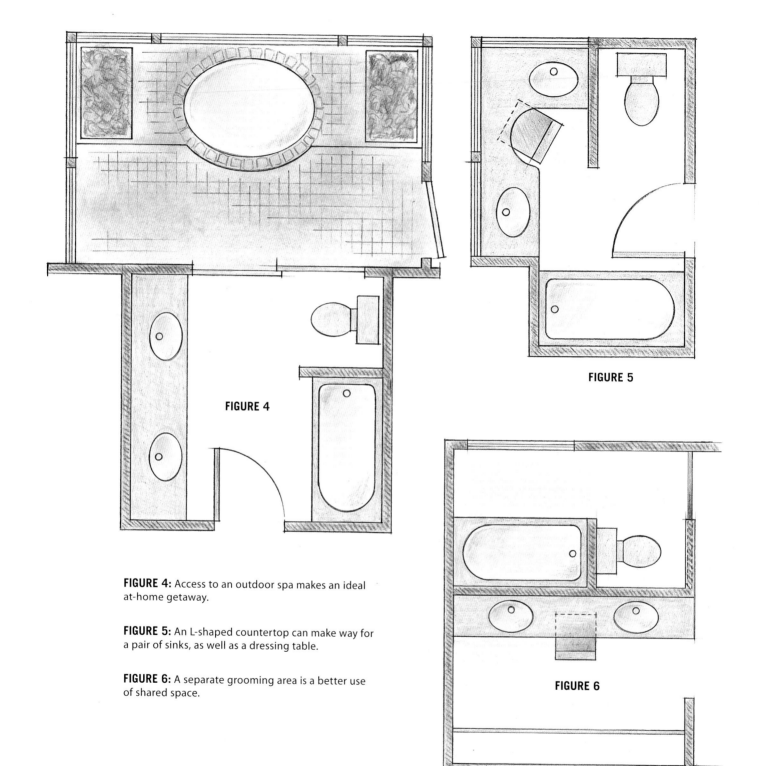

FIGURE 4

FIGURE 5

FIGURE 6

FIGURE 4: Access to an outdoor spa makes an ideal at-home getaway.

FIGURE 5: An L-shaped countertop can make way for a pair of sinks, as well as a dressing table.

FIGURE 6: A separate grooming area is a better use of shared space.

TOP: Natural materials and a fireplace complement the outdoor views of this en suite bath.

RIGHT: A well-lit grooming area offers a private and relaxing place to start the morning.

BOTTOM: This charming bath was built for relaxing after a day on the water or on the slopes. Double pedestal sinks allowed the homeowners to prioritize a large jetted tub along the adjacent wall.

A "wet platform" at the far end of this cabin-inspired bath contains a double shower and custom-built soaking tub. Wood furnishings and trim warm up the cool stone.

FAR RIGHT: Two barely noticeable glass panels enclose the shower to prevent spray. This frameless installation offers an unobstructed view of the room's stylish endpoint—and the lush landscapes outside.

it's in the DETAILS

TOP RIGHT: To enhance the theme, the homeowners selected pebble-tile flooring for the bathing area. A slab of stone from the property serves as a unique step up into the bathtub.

BOTTOM RIGHT: In the shower, separate showerheads and diverters allow two people showering together to choose their own water temperature and spray pattern.

Planning Shared Spaces

When families share a bath, creating an organized layout that serves all members of the household is important, especially when there are kids or older adults involved. Elements should be comfortable for all to use. In the shower, a handheld sprayer that a child can easily reach is a good idea. Both children and adults will find lever-style valves easier to operate than knobs or cross handles. Most localities require installing faucets with anti-scald devices. Use them, and make sure the water temperature is set at a level that won't scald tender skin.

If you can, divide the space into distinct grooming, bathing, and toileting areas—this will increase privacy and alleviate some of the issues that come up when sharing a space with multiple people. Double sinks will help the space to be more efficient during busy times as well. If at all possible, plan to provide storage for everyone's things—from toiletries to towels and even bath-time toys. This will keep surfaces like tub and bathroom floors free from unnecessary clutter that can cause slip and fall accidents.

Because kids grow, it's usually not practical to build shorter vanities. But you can consider a vanity with a convenient space underneath to slip a step stool. If you don't have room for a dressing table, a wall-mount vanity can provide similar open space below.

In a busy bath, go with easy-to-clean fixtures and materials—like these undermount sinks, sleek cabinet doors, and a mirrored backsplash panel.

Family Bath Design Options

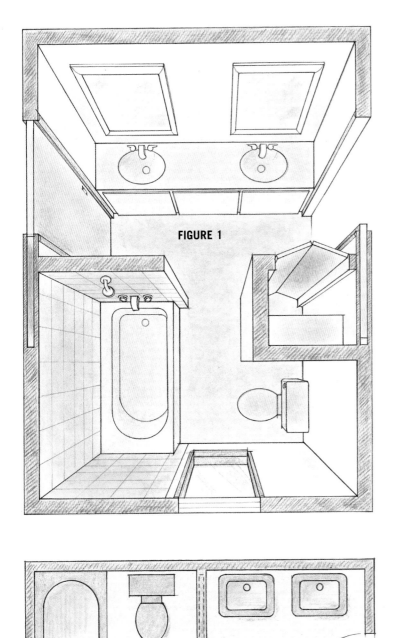

FIGURE 1

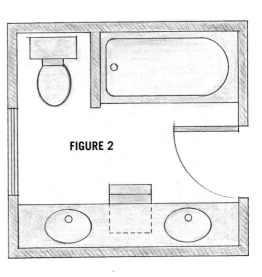

FIGURE 2

FIGURE 1: Pocket doors, installed around this room, do not use up floor space, allowing for an improved floor plan.

FIGURE 2: A partition next to the toilet provides a bit more privacy without a costly addition.

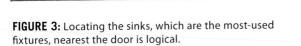

FIGURE 3

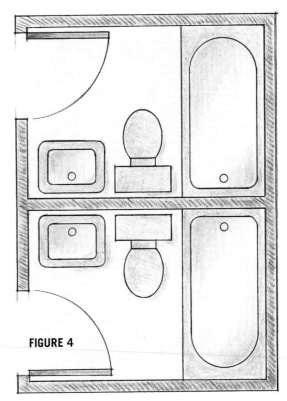

FIGURE 4

FIGURE 3: Locating the sinks, which are the most-used fixtures, nearest the door is logical.

FIGURE 4: Back-to-back plumbing creates two smaller bathrooms from one formerly large space.

Q&A

What can I do to make sure my bathroom is a place that my family can use for years?

what the experts say

Universal design is a concept that aims to ensure anyone can use a space, regardless of age, size, and physical or cognitive ability. This includes anticipating needs as you age (sometimes called "aging in place") and the needs of guests in your home. These guidelines touch on everything from recommended widths for doorways, to how high (or low) to place a towel bar and how much floor space should be available to accommodate a wheelchair. This is where professionals with accessibility and aging specialties can really help.

what real people do

It's easier to prioritize accessibility when you're building a new bath or committing to a major renovation. Existing baths, especially small ones, can be tricky. But there's plenty of thoughtful design choices that are relatively easy to incorporate. Switch to D-shaped hardware pulls to make cabinet doors and drawers easier to open. Another practical change is to swap cross-handle and knob faucet handles and tub/shower controls for models with lever handles. In both cases, someone with limited hand strength or mobility can more easily use the space. It helps to make sure that hot and cold are clearly indicated on faucets and shower valves, too.

One of the biggest impacts in the bathroom is a zero-threshold shower (turn the page for an example). These showers rely on a subtle floor slope to run water toward the drain, thus eliminating the need for the curb that's common to many walk-in showers. Even just a couple inches can pose a tripping hazard or a barrier for someone with a mobility device.

D-shaped cabinet hardware and lever faucets make this vanity easier for all to use.

A well-lit bath is important for safety—motion activated lights and smart lighting controls have benefits for every stage of life. And don't forget to make sure light switches are reachable.

54   THE SMART APPROACH TO DESIGN: BATHROOMS

GET SMART

Universal design isn't all or nothing. While a full bath on the main level of your home is recommended, even a powder room is a helpful step in the right direction when there's otherwise no bathroom accessible without climbing stairs.

Level up your shower. A handheld shower lets you direct water where you need it, from avoiding your hair to avoiding bandages; grab bars provide safe support.

Separated, but not closed off, this bright bath lives large. It confines the grooming area to the corner away from the toilet and situates storage—including the linen closet and built-in storage in the corner opposite—to one convenient area of the room.

FAR RIGHT: Mosaic floor tiles offer traction in the bath, while brick wall tiles keep the shower looking elegant. This is a zero-threshold shower, so there's no curb to step over to enter and exit.

it's in the DETAILS

TOP RIGHT: Walls, rather than doors, help compartmentalize the areas of this bath. Forgoing doors when possible makes a small or narrow space easier to navigate so it's safer and more accessible. Notice the grab bar for support at the toilet as well as in the shower.

BOTTOM RIGHT: A deep blue vanity is a welcome contrast to the many light shades of blue in the room. Varying shades, shapes, and textures is key in a monochromatic bath.

DESIGN BY GOLDEN RULE BUILDERS, PHOTOGRAPHY BY KAAN OZTURK.

Partial Baths

Technically speaking, a bath with a shower but no tub is called a three-quarter bath. Many homeowners choose this over a full bath because they prefer showering, or they simply don't have the space for a tub in the room. These baths are also popular for creating spacious walk-in showers with fancy amenities. These layouts have enormous variety and can be used in baths, both spacious or compact.

Half baths, also called powder rooms, have only a toilet and sink. Powder rooms require little space, and you can often find small-scale fixtures intended to outfit these petite baths. Door swing and plumbing locations are two of the biggest impacts on how the space is laid out.

Corner fixtures help you fit more in a small space and often give you more room to move around. The small sink (bottom left) and rounded shower (bottom right) tuck into the corner in order to not encroach on someone using the toilet.

Half and Three-Quarter Baths

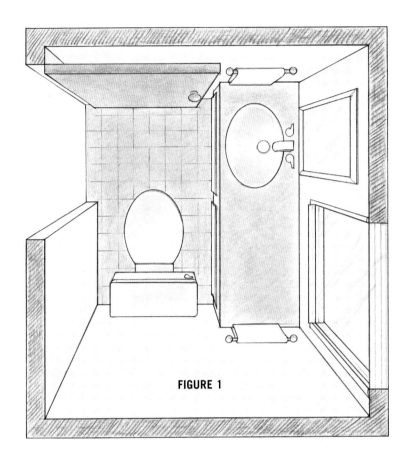

FIGURE 1

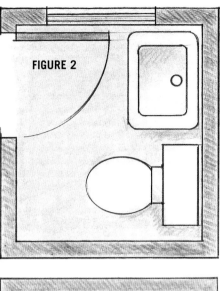

FIGURE 2

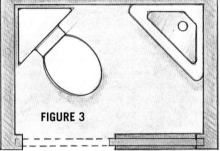

FIGURE 3

FIGURE 1: A large vanity is helpful if a half bath doubles as an extra grooming area on busy mornings.

FIGURE 2: Locate the sink and the toilet on the same wall to conserve floor space.

FIGURE 3: Corner fixtures and a pocket door are small-space solutions.

FIGURE 4: A corner shower unit can convert a half bath into a three-quarter bath.

FIGURE 5: In a long, narrow room, place the toilet and the sink on opposite walls.

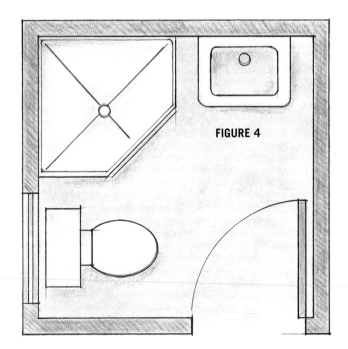

FIGURE 4

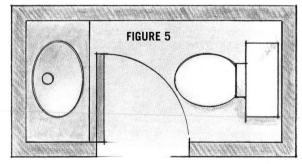

FIGURE 5

Planning for Guests

Half and three-quarter layouts are common arrangements for guest baths. Want to make a guest bath stand out? Include both luxurious and practical elements. For example, splurge on a fancy toilet or bidet seat and a heated towel bar, and add motion-sense lighting so no one is feeling around to find light switches. Also incorporate elements to help friends and family staying overnight: toe kick lighting or a backlit mirror that dims can help them navigate the space at night, while a toothbrush holder keeps their toothbrushes off the countertop. Little details and thoughtful planning pamper guests, whether they're in your home for two hours or two weeks.

2. PATTERN

4. NIP AND TUCK

TOP 10
Half Bath Tips

Going into the project with a clear, detailed picture will help a big project run smoothly.

1. COLOR. Even if you feel timid about using deep colors elsewhere, go for it here. Kick it up a notch with a mix of matte and high-gloss finishes.

8. CHOOSE GLAMOUR

2. PATTERN. Bold pattern in a tiny room? Absolutely! Use oversize wallpaper and fabric patterns. Large prints make big statements, and your powder room will look grand.

3. ROUND IT OUT. Curved or round furnishings take the boxy look out of a small space.

4. NIP AND TUCK. Extend a portion of the vanity counter over a toilet tank.

5. GO HANDS-FREE. Touchless faucets and lighting help half baths stay cleaner.

6. INSTALL A PEDESTAL SINK. A pedestal sink is pretty, and it makes good use of small space.

7. INCLUDE GOOD LIGHTING. Remember, your guests may be using the powder room to touch up makeup or take medicine—make sure there's adequate lighting.

8. CHOOSE GLAMOUR. Splurge on special fixtures: a small chandelier, a hand-painted lav, or gorgeous fittings.

9. USE AN ANTIQUE. Swap a standard vanity and retrofit an old table, cabinet, or chest with a lav and faucet to create a unique style statement that's also perfect for your small space.

10. PLAN FOR STORAGE. When possible, make it easier on yourself by planning a space to conceal toilet brush, plunger, and other less attractive necessities.

Basement, Attic, and Closet Baths

Adding a bathroom to a basement, attic, or place in the home that isn't already prepped for one can be major work—not to mention costly. But there are ways to make the work easier, and less expensive, to help you get the job done.

Remodeling a basement to add a bath often requires major construction, like drilling into the concrete to add a drain. Location is also typically limited by existing plumbing. Some products can help you build a bath with less hassle in these unfinished spaces. Saniflo products, for example, use pumps that move waste from the bath to the main sewer lines—which can be more than 100 feet away—to give you the flexibility to install a sink, shower, and even toilet without drilling into floors or tethering tightly to existing plumbing. It's a smart solution for adding a basement bath without some of the major work.

A macerating toilet utilizes a macerator to grind waste and a pump to move the waste, against gravity, up to your main plumbing stack (they're also called upflush toilets). It's a smart solution for adding a basement bath without the major work, and expense, of breaking into the concrete floor for plumbing. There are similar products for moving greywater from a shower and sink as well. But these systems are not just for basements—they can also help bring a bath to an area of the home away from the main plumbing, like converting a closet to a powder room. Another benefit: if you have the materials and easy access to the main stack, this kind of system can be added in a weekend.

If you're finishing an attic to include a bedroom, a bathroom is an appealing addition. It will require careful planning—from choosing the best location based on your home's existing plumbing, to verifying the floor can carry the weight of the new space. Licensed professionals will be critical.

Macerating toilets and waste pumps are compact units that can be hidden inside vanity cabinets, under a raised shower floor, tucked behind a toilet, or placed behind the wall before drywall is in place.

GET SMART
LOCATION, LOCATION, LOCATION

The easiest and least-expensive remodels take advantage of the existing water supplies, drain lines, and vent stacks. If you want to add a bath, try locating it next to an existing one and lower your costs.

Adding a shower to an attic—or any room affected by eaves and roof lines—is a matter of creative floor planning. Where ceiling height is impacted most, toilets and tubs may be a great fit. Showers and standing areas, in front of a vanity for example, should be positioned in areas of the room with more clearance.

Tub and shower surround kits that make it very easy to install impervious walls (that require little care and maintenance!) to quickly and inexpensively add a shower. Prefabricated shower stalls made of acrylic and fiberglass are common. Also popular are modular glass shower enclosures. These time-saving options are typically budget-friendly selections, too, but note that the lower the price, the fewer style offerings. It's important to make sure that they're installed well so you don't have to be concerned about mold, leaks, or water getting behind the enclosure.

Look into shower basins and tub models meant for above floor rough-in plumbing. By lifting the shower tray, or tub, a few inches off the main floor, the fixture can sit on top of the current floor with room to run pipes to existing plumbing for drainage—this may save you from having to break into the current floor or jackhammer into the unfinished basement floor in order to set up plumbing. Fixtures that accommodate above floor rough-in plumbing can sometimes help reconfigure an existing bath for new fixtures or a different layout, as well.

Instead of spending time and money building out shower walls and then tiling them, a prefabricated unit can provide walls and even a shower floor or tub. It saves on resources for a bath in any room of the home, not just basements and attics.

Above floor rough-in plumbing can be found for both freestanding and built-in tubs. The plumbing is hidden within the platform constructed for the drop-in tub, or behind the tub's apron or on floor-mounted and alcove models.

CHAPTER 3

Outfitting Your Bath

Tubs, toilets, showers, sinks, and faucets are the fundamental components of the bath. The fixtures and fittings in today's bathrooms can be described as luxurious, hardworking, and eco-conscious. Some are technologically advanced, too, connecting to smart home devices and incorporating Bluetooth, lighting, and other features. Not just a place to start and end the day, primary baths are making room for wellness and relaxation. As a result, we're seeing spaces that provide rejuvenating and spa-like experiences at home.

Function is always the most important consideration, but style sways our choices. The variety of finishes, features and design options will allow you to express your personal style and create a custom bathing experience.

Q&A

I'm ready to choose fixtures for my new bathroom, but I don't know where to begin. What will look right in my space?

what the experts say

Interior designer Helene Goodman, IIDA, says, "Consider the style and setting of your home. If it's contemporary, for instance, choose fixtures that complement that style." Geometric shapes, hard angles, and clean lines are hallmarks of this look, while embellishments such as fluting and other classical details are more traditional. "Getting advice from a qualified interior designer could save you a costly mistake and time."

what real people do

"Typically, homeowners are willing to spend more on a primary bathroom because this space will receive the most use on a daily basis," says Goodman. But the powder room is always a good place to do something a little different. It is not necessary to match the color of the sink to that of the toilet. Many of her clients, for example, choose a powder-room sink made of glass, metal, or stone.

Sometimes just choosing the right fittings can establish a look. Case in point: Jack and Elaine bought their new house because it was "move-in ready," they said. The primary bath was "souped up and ultra-modern," but it seemed too "industrial-looking and cold" for their traditional taste. Rather than ripping out all of the fixtures, they swapped the polished chrome fittings for ones with an oil-rubbed bronze finish. Voilà! Instant warmth.

Bath Fixtures

For big renovations or new construction, the options are almost limitless. If you're looking for light remodeling, your choices may be limited by the current bath's setup: replacing a faucet or showerhead with a model that uses similar installation will certainly be easier than potentially replacing a countertop or redoing a shower wall, too. But there are plenty of opportunities to get a stylish update and better-functioning space.

Water, and its consumption, is on everybody's mind. Toilets account for about 30 percent of residential water usage, and showers use about 37 percent. Add onto that the energy used by your water heater to maintain the perfect temperature, and it's easy to see how water use and energy efficiency are big factors when it comes to bath fixtures. Thankfully, it's easy to find high-performing and efficient fixtures that also look good—just look for the Environmental Protection Agency's "WaterSense" label when you're shopping. These products use at least 20 percent less water while performing as well as, or better than, their standard counterparts.

Don't worry about sacrificing looks for function—in today's world, you can have both. Fixtures and fittings that suit your modern taste or your traditional leanings abound. You can even combine them! You'll find them fabricated in materials, shapes, and finishes as glamorous as any baubles you might see on the red carpet.

9. SMART TOILETS AND BIDET SEATS

TOP 10
Fixture Amenities

Products that promote better hygiene, increase safety, and encourage relaxation are topping the list when it comes to outfitting your bath.

1. Smart controls are giving us access to everything—from shower temperatures to lighting settings and floor heat—through wall-mounted digital interfaces, remote controls, voice control, and even app control (so you can start your shower from bed). Many allow personalized settings, so you know that shower will be just the right temperature and spray setting.

2. Shower seats of all kinds are sneaking into the space, including permanent benches, removable stools, and wall-mount fold-down seats. They provide support and relaxation.

3. Touchless faucets continue gaining ground after the pandemic. They're easy to use, easy to clean, and collect fewer germs.

6. LINEAR SHOWER DRAINS

10. HANDHELD SHOWERHEADS

7. SPA FEATURES

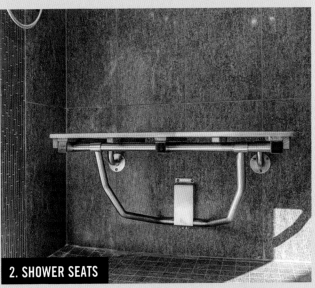

2. SHOWER SEATS

4. Grab bars help with balance and supporting weight, especially in the shower and near the toilet. They used to appear cold and institutional, but now, they're a common part of bathroom planning, thanks to universal design.

5. Easy-to-clean and maintain fixtures like undermount and integrated sinks, or finishes that don't show as many spots or fingerprints. Matte and brushed finishes are most popular in the bath. Instead of stone, wood, and glass for sinks and tubs, materials that require less maintenance are preferred.

6. Linear shower drains have a clean look that can integrate into a shower's floor material to be almost seamless. More importantly, they maximize drainage with their length.

7. Spa features create ultra-relaxing and luxurious bathing experiences. These features can include spacious, steam-equipped showers, multiple body sprays, soaking tubs, and even chromotherapy or aromatherapy.

8. Curbless showers are creating barrier-free bathing for people of all ages and abilities.

9. Smart toilets and bidet seats promote good hygiene. Though there are standalone bidets, they're most commonly found as an add-on seat to an existing toilet, making them an easy but luxurious upgrade. It's likely these smart toilets and bidets will require an electrical outlet nearby.

10. Handheld showerheads have never been off the radar, but they're more prevalent than ever. Sometimes they're the main source of water, but often they're a supplement.

Soaking in Style

Soakers; whirlpools; classic claw-footed models; tubs for two; spas for four; contoured shapes, ovals, squares, or rounded tubs; streamlined or sculptured models; jetted tubs; tubs that offer a bubble massage; or a holistic-healing-inspired bath that incorporates sound, vibration, and chromotherapy. Hey, it's your soak, so have it your way.

Tubs can be custom-made of stone, concrete, copper, and even wood, but standard models are typically fabricated out of one of the following materials:

FIBERGLASS. Lightweight and moldable, a fiberglass tub is the least expensive type you can buy. But it's prone to scratching and wear after about a dozen years. Some come with an acrylic finish, which holds up against wear longer.

SOLID ACRYLIC. A mid-price product, acrylic is more durable than fiberglass and less prone to scratching because the color is solid all the way through. Whirlpool tubs are usually made of acrylic because it can be shaped easily. It's also lightweight, an important feature for large tubs that can put stress on structural elements under the floor.

CAST-IRON. An enamel-coated cast-iron tub will endure as long as your house stands. It's a heavyweight, though, and isn't recommended for a large soaking tub unless there's adequate support.

The most common size for a tub that backs up against a wall is 32 x 60 inches, but you can find models in widths of 24 to 42 inches. If someone in the family is tall, no problem: you can purchase a standard tub that's up to 72 inches long.

There are four common tub types. Alcove tubs have walls on three sides—these are common tub/shower combinations. Drop-in and under-mount tubs require a tub surround to house the unit. Freestanding tubs sit anywhere in the room and the entire fixture is visible.

GET SMART SPA LUXURY

Whirlpools and jetted tubs were once the main way to get a spa-like bathing experience at home. Now, there are more options than ever for getting a deluxe soak from the comfort of your primary bath—from air and water jets to steam, aromatherapy, and chromotherapy. Not all tubs will have the same features, but the more you're willing to spend, the more you can bring home. So, dim the lights, put on soothing music, heat your towels, and check out the features available on today's soaking tubs.

This infinity tub utilizes water, light and fog—even aromas, if essential oils are your thing—to truly bring the spa experience into your primary bathroom. Water flows over the sides of the tub, offering a soothing ambient sound and visible water feature.

Q&A

I'm doing a small bathroom renovation and my bathtub is badly stained. Can I repair it, or should I replace it?

what the experts say

Folks at the National Kitchen and Bath Association (NKBA) advise checking with the manufacturer of the unit; sometimes stains are not as egregious as they seem. Also look into the construction of the unit: if it is in two or more pieces—like an acrylic tub and shower surround—you may be able to replace only a portion of it. If the problem is on the walls of an acrylic unit, though, the NKBA suggests replacing the wall section or replacing the surround entirely with something like tile.

what real people do

A new tub isn't necessarily expensive, but once you factor in the cost of installing it (and removing the old one), you can blow a sizable chunk of your budget. An alternative is to install a tub liner. This involves applying a form-fitting acrylic sheet, or liner, over the old tub. The installer takes detailed measurements of your tub to fabricate a seamless match. Upon installation, a special adhesive binds the liner to the tub without disturbing the adjacent walls and existing plumbing.

Another solution for minor chips or cracks in enameled or porcelainized tubs is reglazing. There are some refinishing products and kits for confident DIYers, too. For a beloved fixture with special character that has seen better days, like a vintage cast-iron tub, look into professional refinishing. This can include filling in cracks and scratches before re-enameling— however, it won't necessarily be a budget-friendly choice.

The material type of your bathtub, as well as its condition and location, will help you determine if it can be cleaned, refinished, or replaced. Refinishing the exterior of a cast-iron tub can be an opportunity to update the body to a fresh new color.

Tub Faucets and Fillers

There are four standard options for filling a tub. You need a **FREESTANDING** model when you want a big dramatic tub in the middle of a room—they're mounted to the floor. **WALL-MOUNT** fillers are the style you're used to seeing in most tub-shower combos. **DECK-MOUNT** faucets fill from their location on the tub surround, while **TUB-MOUNT** fillers are attached to the tub itself.

Whether your style is modern or traditional, you can outfit your tub and shower with faucets and fittings to match. You can select from an array of trendy finishes—from highly polished to satin matte in chrome, nickel, pewter, brass, bronze, black, and even rose gold. Two-tone styles are also an option.

With any of these traditionally mounted fillers, it's common to incorporate a handheld sprayer. It not only offers shower-like cleaning from a tub, but it's also ideal for bathing children and pets.

Looking for something a bit different? You can find tubs that fill from the bottom, or go for drama with a filler mounted from the ceiling. This streamlined design is a shower with a tub filler all in one unit; this Japanese soaking tub has a faucet that produces a waterfall effect.

Bathrooms designed to please are those with high-quality fixtures and fittings that are both beautiful and reliable.

FAR RIGHT: A glamorous, deep soaking tub is the focal point of this primary bathroom, taking center stage in front of a windowed alcove. Separate lavs and vanities on either side create perfect symmetry.

it's in the
DETAILS

TOP RIGHT: Note the tub's elegant French-style "telephone" faucet. Its sprayer handle is both practical and charming.

BOTTOM RIGHT: The glass-enclosed jetted shower features both a fixed showerhead and handheld sprayers.

Praiseworthy Showers

Increasing shower size has been a significant remodeling trend, according to research from the NKBA. To make it happen, some homeowners are removing tubs from their primary baths altogether. Customize your shower with all or some of today's pampering extras, including massaging jets, steam, natural light, and music. Build a space for two, or plan with aging in mind, or keep it all fairly traditional. The only thing limiting your showering experience is your imagination—and perhaps, your budget. Here are a couple shower features for you to consider.

Steam showers require a steam generator connected to a water supply. They should be fully enclosed for maximum efficiency (steam buildup), and the shower walls should be tightly sealed to protect them from the extra moisture. Controls are typically digital and accessible in the shower, so you can set temperature and other features.

When it comes to bathing, barrier-free showers are the most accessible design. Unlike a tub/shower combo or a traditional shower, a curbless shower doesn't have a raised threshold you must step over to enter the shower, so it's safe and easy to enter whether you're using a walker, a wheelchair, or without assistance. To keep water from exiting the shower, a sloped shower floor replaces the curb, so when it comes to remodeling, there will be additional costs and preparations needed for installation.

BOTTOM LEFT: Not surprisingly, two-person showers are a popular configuration for today's larger showers.

BOTTOM RIGHT: This shower bench below a skylight provides an enticing place to relax.

LEFT: Not only is this shower entry curbless, it's also doorless, which is great for accessibility. It also means you don't have to worry about door swing when fitting in the rest of the bath's fixtures and storage.

BOTTOM: Steam showers don't have to be grand. This standard-sized shower has everything it needs to deliver a steamy experience, too.

Showerheads and Sprays

Customize your shower with all or some of today's pampering extras, including massaging jets, steam, natural light, and music. Unless you're interested in a strictly no-frills unit, think about installing more than one showerhead and mixing and matching devices from any or all of the following basic spray categories.

FIXED SPRAY. Attached to a shower arm and mounted to the wall or ceiling, fixed sprays can have a large head and spray area. These showerheads often include multiple spray patterns and may come with a massage option. Rain style showers are popular because they pamper you with a soft rinse from above.

HANDHELD SPRAY. A handheld device is convenient for directing water where you want it. It's connected to a wall-mounted slide bar that can be adjusted up and down to accommodate the tallest or shortest bather—a perk when multiple family members of varied heights use the same shower. It can also be mounted and used like a traditional fixed spray showerhead, but on a removable cradle.

BODY SPRAYS. Like those used in whirlpool tubs, shower water- and air-jet sprays are housed behind the shower walls. Use just a couple on one wall, or multiple sprays on different walls to wrap yourself in water coming from all directions, and create an environment for a relaxing, full-body spray or a more intense, therapeutic hydromassage to relax stiff neck muscles or a sore back.

GO GREEN

Looking for a low-flow showerhead that uses less water? There are two types. Aerating heads work by incorporating air into the water flow. Non-aerating models with laminar flow heads form powerful individual streams of water.

ABOVE: Black is a popular fixture finish that didn't have the same cachet a few years ago. Now, you can find black fixtures in an array of styles.

RIGHT: In spa-like showers, multiple showerheads can be used at once, or just one at a time. In open showers like this, the varied sources can help keep you feeling warm.

If you currently don't have a ceiling-mount showerhead, you can still get the rainfall experience. Pair a long arm and a rain style showerhead.

With a ceiling-mount rain showerhead at one end and wall-mount showerhead and handheld shower at the other, this two-person shower was built with universal design in mind.

FAR RIGHT TOP: Textured glass provides plenty of privacy while also allowing light into the large shower.

FAR RIGHT BOTTOM: A shower built for any user doesn't have to look institutional. This space mixes tile types while also coordinating the shower frame and plumbing fixtures with the sink and cabinet hardware and other accessories in the rest of the bath. Also notice the recessed niche and shower controls that are located at a lower, more universally accessible height.

it's in the DETAILS

TOP RIGHT: A barrier-free entry means there is a smooth transition from outside the shower to inside the shower. Linear drains at either end of the shower collect the water so it doesn't run out. The entry is 32 inches wide—the minimum width for ADA compliance.

BOTTOM RIGHT: Want to relax? Need assistance? A shower seat can help. A removable seat like this is convenient so that it can be easily positioned in the best spot for the user, or removed entirely to make room for an assistive mobility device.

Superb Sinks

Sinks, also called lavs, can be made of vitreous china, cast-iron, enameled steel, glass, solid-surfacing material, stone, faux stone, metal, or even wood. Its finish may be hand painted, contoured, beveled, brushed, or polished. They may be traditionally rounded, sleek, and square, or even modern custom shapes. The choice is yours.

Because sinks function the same, your selection will likely be based on aesthetics or maintenance. Some materials require sealing or are more prone to damage; others are easy-to-clean workhorses. When it comes to installation, there are a few traditional options.

VESSEL. A vessel lav is an above-counter installation that sits much like a bowl on a table. But a lav that's installed into a vanity counter is described in one of four ways:

SELF-RIMMING. Also called a drop-in sink, the bowl of a self-rimming sink is surface-mounted: you drop it into the counter, and the ridge forms a seal with the countertop surface.

RIMMED. Unlike a self-rimming lav, this type requires a metal strip to form the seal between the top of the sink and the countertop.

UNDER-MOUNTED. If you want a neat, modern look that's also easy to clean, an under-mounted sink may be for you. In this instance, the bowl is attached underneath the countertop for a sleek, uncluttered appearance.

INTEGRAL. As the word "integral" implies, the sink and countertop are fabricated from the same material, such as stone or solid surfacing. The look is seamless and sculptural.

LEFT: Lavs come in all sizes and shapes. This integrated sink and floating vanity countertop has a distinctly modern feel.

This thick-edged drop-in sink is traditional, as is the under-mount polished stainless-steel bowl elegantly paired with white marble.

The softened form of this vessel sink helps it match any style.

A pedestal sink is a classic style that works especially well in a small room because it doesn't take up too much physical or visual space. The graphic backdrop of the wallpaper really helps show off its shape, too.

Lav Faucets

Faucets might work hard, but they can look good, too. Much like tub and shower fixtures, they come in an array of finishes and styles. If you're looking for something different to stand out, you may find crystal or porcelain handle accents, two-tone finishes, or waterfall spouts. Matte and brushed finishes are less shiny—and typically easier to keep looking clean, so they're more popular, too—but polished finishes are eye-catching and common.

There are three basic types of faucets for your consideration:

CENTER-SET FAUCETS have two separate valves (one for hot, another for cold) and a spout that are connected in one unit.

WIDESPREAD FAUCETS feature a spout with separate hot- and cold-water valves. All appear to be completely separate pieces.

SINGLE-LEVER FAUCETS have a spout and a single lever in one piece.

And don't forget about **TOUCHLESS FAUCETS**, which are becoming more common.

Installation is also a factor when choosing a faucet. Will it be mounted on the wall, on the sink, or on the countertop? Of course, the faucet will need to coordinate with the sink.

TOP: With custom countertops and cabinetry, you can choose the installation types.

LEFT: It's okay to have fun with your faucets. A whimsical shape is a detail your guests will notice.

GET SMART ACCESS FOR ALL

When you're choosing a style, consider where the faucet will be installed and who could be using it. According to universal design principles, faucets should be usable with only one hand and should not require a lot of twisting. Cross handles are charming, but they can be difficult to grasp; a single-lever faucet allows the user to turn water off and on with an open palm or a closed fist.

Efficient Toilets

Though there are more distinct and colorful options available, a simple and elegant white toilet will go with any style bathroom. From high-tech marvels to traditional two-pieces or sleek tankless units, toilets are more efficient than ever. Dual flush toilets debuted in the 1980s and are quickly becoming a common feature. They offer two flushing options: a partial flush, which releases a small volume of water for flushing liquid and paper waste; or a larger flush, which releases a greater volume of water for flushing solid waste.

Comfort is a key factor in selecting the best toilet. Toilet height is measured from the floor to the rim of the toilet, including the seat: standard toilet seats are 14 to 15 inches off the ground, while "chair-height" toilets usually fit in the ADA-compliant range of 17 to 19 inches. These taller toilets are generally easier for folks to get on and off. Elongated bowls are oval and have more sitting area than a rounded bowl, making them more comfortable for some users. But with an added two inches in depth, elongated bowls take up more space, too, which can lead to obstructed door swings and knee bumps in small baths.

Cleaning and maintenance also play a big part in decision making. Two-piece models, with a separate tank that bolts onto the bowl, are often cheaper than one-piece toilets, but they can be harder to clean due to the seam between the two pieces. Skirted toilets are the easiest to maintain because they lack visible traps and bolts.

GO GREEN

If your existing toilet was installed before the mid-1990s, it's time for a change. The federal standard now requires toilets use 1.6 gallons of water or less per flush, but according to the EPA, advancements have allowed toilets to use only 1.28 gallons per flush while providing equal performance.

Toilets with visible trapways—the bends and curves visible on the back of the toilet—are more difficult to keep clean than models with trapways concealed behind smooth sides.

Lever flushes are familiar, but they're not the only options. Here, dual flush controls are found on top of the toilet tank and mounted above the wall-hung toilet. The floating toilet includes a bidet attachment with a separate remote.

SMART APPROACH: GET THE BEST BUY

CONSIDER THE TIMING

If you're sprucing up an old bath or adding a new one in a house that you expect to sell soon, you might install fixtures with fewer bells and whistles. But if you're making a major investment, you will be happier in the long run with fixtures that may cost more, but give you greater satisfaction for years to come.

GO FOR QUALITY

Sure, style is important, but it's just as easy to find a first-rate faucet that looks great in your new bathroom as it is to find one that looks fabulous, but performs poorly. Always put quality first. Check the manufacturer details and look into the expected life of the product, as well as its efficiency and interior construction. For example, the best choice for faucets are solid brass or a brass-metal base, which are corrosion-resistant. Avoid plastic—it won't hold up.

SEEK ADVICE

Not sure about some deluxe features and whether they're
worth the extra dollars you'll have to spend? Research
product feedback on the Internet. Talk to your contractor,
designer, or another professional who may be familiar with it,
or who can pass along critical feedback from others who may
have purchased the same item or something similar to it.

Finding two similar faucets at drastically different
prices and not sure why? Check with a professional.

THINK GREEN

When investing in substantial fixtures for your bath, you
can feel good about making informed decisions. Energy-
and water-efficient models aren't just environmental
hype—they'll help you save on your bills, too. Shopping
for items with a WaterSense Label is a great way to know
you'll get performance and efficiency.

CHAPTER 4

SURFACES

Walls, countertops, and flooring require special attention in the bath. These coverings need to hold up against frequent use, withstand humidity and water, and support bath safety. Ideally, they're also good looking and easy to maintain.

From floor tiles to shower surrounds, these are arguably the hardest working elements of your bath—and some of the hardest to make decisions about, too. In this chapter, you'll find a fair sampling of what you can expect when you start shopping, plus advice for choosing materials that will serve you well.

It's great to have choices, but how to narrow them down? Start with what works best for your lifestyle.

It's a Cover Story

Ceramic tile was once practically the only game in town, but now there's a dizzying array of colors and materials: stone, wood, glass, concrete, solid surfacing, and even remarkable materials made to look like other materials, such as wood-look porcelain plank tiles. Durability, safety, and style—it's okay to expect a lot from your surfaces! Just make sure to do your research and pick the right material for the surface: unless you're updating paint colors, surfaces aren't that easy to change if you aren't happy with them, and they cost a lot more than a gallon of paint, too.

2. NATURAL PATTERNS AND TEXTURES

TOP 10
Surface Trends

1. Glass shower screens protect the bath from water spray while letting light in.

2. Natural patterns and textures like wood grain and marble veining are big for walls, floors, and countertops.

Surfaces aren't just a protective covering. Here, a stunning strip of sintered stone runs along the floor, wall, and ceiling, drawing you toward the end of the room and showcasing the vanity area.

3. HANDMADE TILES

9. INTEGRATED SINKS AND COUNTERTOPS

3. Handmade tiles, and tiles that only look artisanal, lend warmth and dimension to walls and floors.

4. Light countertops reflect ambient light and complement both wood-tone and painted vanities in any style bath.

5. More windows are increasing natural light in the bath, which means less wall space for you to cover.

6. Radiant heat flooring is warming up new floors in spaces of all sizes, especially in primary baths.

7. Porcelain flooring is the most popular flooring type, especially in wood-look planks.

8. Large-format wall coverings like cladding, slabs, and large tiles, are being chosen for style and function.

9. Integrated sinks and countertops offer a sleek look that's easy to clean.

10. Watery blues and greens are creating a spa-like atmosphere.

Wonderful Walls

Perhaps more than any other room in your home, your bathroom walls offer limitless potential for personalization, from paint to wallpaper, wainscoting, and seemingly endless styles of tile—or a mix of all four.

It's important to consider the proximity to water when selecting wall surfaces. You can get away with something less moisture resistant when it's not, for example, in the shower. But in spaces large and small, moisture easily condenses on other walls and ceilings from hot showers and baths. And there are splashes to contend with, too.

Another consideration is cleaning. Are you willing to wipe down walls after a shower or seal grout for long-lasting wear? Care and maintenance are key reasons that large-format tiles, cladding, and slab walls (panel style coverings) are in high demand. These options have fewer, thinner grout lines, making them easier to clean while also better protecting walls from moisture.

Light surfaces reflect light, and dark colors absorb light; use this to your advantage. Dark and dramatic walls are most successful if you balance them with natural light and some light-colored surfaces like flooring and countertops, or even a tub.

Mirrored walls are a big part of designs invoking Hollywood regency glam. They're great for reflecting natural light and helping a small space feel larger, but they need to be frequently cleaned of water spots, handprints, and dust.

Slate's natural color variations and rugged texture give this wall an added layer of interest. It brings a sense of the outdoors into a bath with a lake view.

CERAMIC tiles are the classic way to dress up (and protect) walls. Porcelain is a popular type of ceramic tile, and both are nearly impervious to water, durable, and don't require maintenance. They're ideal for showers and walls in small, humid bathrooms. Made from clay, they're available in a profusion of shapes and colors, and the variety means you can find ceramic and porcelain in every style of bath, and at varied price points, too.

Another staple of bathroom design, **GLASS** tiles also come in many colors, often with multiple shades mixed together. Some are iridescent, but all are luminous and gorgeous. Impervious to moisture, glass doesn't have to be sealed. They're commonly installed in bricks and mosaic patterns.

Although ceramic and glass tiles don't require maintenance, they do typically require grout (the compound that fills the joints) which does need care and attention. Grout is vulnerable to water, so sealing grout is necessary, and squeegeeing shower walls is common. But grout is an important part of the tile's aesthetic, too. Grout can be mixed in a number of colors and installed in different widths, depending on the look you're going for.

White stone subway tiles with matching grout blends so smoothly you almost don't notice the tiled wall. In another space, brown ceramic tiles rely on a lighter, contrasting grout to amplify the subway tile pattern.

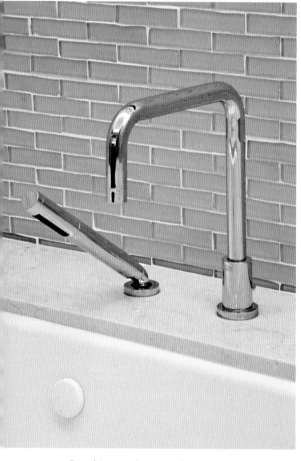

For ultimate glamour, glass is the one. But glass tiles can be expensive, so you might want to use them sparingly, like as a border or accent.

SINTERED STONE is a new, engineered stone material gaining ground in bath design. It's incredibly durable, waterproof, heat resistant, and stain proof. It can be fabricated in cladding, making it a great selection for covering walls or even entire rooms with few seams. But take note: this new material requires knowledgeable professionals for fabrication and installation, and you'd benefit from expert insight when it comes to planning and design as well.

The popularity of earthy, organic and biophilic design styles means baths are seeing more **WOOD** on walls. It's true that wood does have the potential to be damaged by water and moisture. But when properly sealed with a water-resistant finish, such as polyurethane, wood can hold up fine in a bathroom.

CONCRETE offers a world of decorative possibilities. Concrete's surface can be colored, inlaid, formed into various shapes, or etched. Because concrete is porous, surfaces made with it require a sealant for protection. Even if properly sealed and installed, some concrete surfaces may crack over time. Concrete isn't expensive, but for the best result, you'll have to hire a professional fabricator, which will drive up the cost.

GET SMART

When working with specialty materials, make sure to check your fabricator's references. Also ask to see examples of installations that have been in place for some time.

Sintered stone can mimic other materials like concrete, limestone, or marble.

Certain wood species, including redwood (pictured), teak, and cedar are naturally more stable and rot-resistant than other species.

In this unique setting, humble concrete looks magnificent.

Don't forget everyday coverings like **PAINT** and **WALLPAPER**, which also add color and texture to walls. If you love a long, hot shower, look for paint with a semi-gloss finish—the slight shine helps resist moisture. You can also find paint manufactured specifically to resist mold and mildew. Wallpaper has become increasingly popular in the bathroom, especially powder rooms where the graphic pattern can make a bold statement. Traditional paper wallpaper can be used in the bath, but vinyl wallpaper has extra protection against the damp environment.

ACCENTS like shiplap, beadboard, and wainscotting are another way to dress up walls. They're largely style choices, but they can help protect walls from splashes and drips. Typically wood, you're likely to find wainscotting tile installations as well.

BOTTOM LEFT: Accents like paneling and beadboard are key for traditional, cottage, and vintage decor.

BOTTOM RIGHT: Paint and wallpaper—and all surfaces—will hold up better in a bath with proper ventilation (see Chapter 6).

Q&A

I have recently installed large porcelain tiles on my new shower walls. What type of tile should I use for the floor?

what the experts say

Instead of complementing large tiles, experts suggest using small tiles on the shower floor for two reasons. First, because small tiles can better accommodate the shower floor's slope toward the drain; large tiles would have to be cut to accommodate the angles that the floor will require to get it to slope. Second, because the smaller tiles have more grout lines, which can offer more traction and better slip resistance.

what real people do

The easiest types of small floor tiles to install come on a sheet. This is a relatively easy project for a DIYer. One- or two-inch tiles that are attached to a 12" x 12" mesh-backed sheet let you get around corners and obstructions easily, such as fixtures, because you can cut the mesh or pull off a tile as needed. There's seldom a need to cut the tile itself, and you don't have to use spacers to create even grout lines.

Hexagon tiles on the shower floor are repeated in an accent strip that runs around the room. Above the strip, square tiles blend into the wall, while below, beveled subway tiles stand out. The glass shower enclosure allows anyone using the room to appreciate these details.

TOP: The floor mosaic complements the larger-format wall tiles and provides traction. A bonus of mosaic tiles is that they can be easier to integrate with shower drains.

BOTTOM: Walls show off natural stone veining, while a pebble-inspired floor offers style and safety in this wet-room style bath.

Fabulous Flooring

Ideally, bathroom floors are both waterproof and slip resistant. Water-resistant materials don't absorb water, which is important for the wear of the material and protection of the floor, but that characteristic also leaves water standing on the surface. To avoid slips and falls, flooring should have traction in both wet and dry conditions.

Start by identifying products specified for flooring use by the manufacturer or retailer. Look for materials that are designated slip-resistant or have a high coefficient of friction (COF) rating. You can also choose an installation with smaller tiles that will require more grout lines, as they offer something for feet to grip as well.

Don't forget radiant heat when considering flooring. Though it does require entirely replacing the floor in a remodel—the heating system must go under the flooring—it can be easily planned for in a new bath. Ceramic, porcelain, and natural stone conduct and retain heat well.

While wood isn't a common flooring choice due to its susceptibility to water, wood-look flooring made of ceramic, porcelain (pictured), and vinyl are incredibly popular.

FIGURE 25

FIGURE 26

Flooring is a fun way to add personality to baths. For a bold approach, you can rely on the tile's shape when installed (Fig. 26), or a graphic pattern directly on the material (and Fig. 25).

GET SMART

Like walls, grout will need to be maintained for flooring. Standing water is a concern, but even walking can take its toll. The key is to routinely sweep it so that you don't grind in loose dirt.

Like walls, **CERAMIC** and **PORCELAIN** tiles are popular for flooring because they're non-porous and easy to clean, but they can also be quite slippery when wet. For flooring, they often have a texture or finish that counterbalances the materials' normally slick surface.

STONE is a beautiful flooring option, but it's often slippery whether it's wet or dry. Pay close attention to finish, installation, and ratings for stone flooring, and don't forget that it likely needs to be sealed for protection.

VINYL is a budget-friendly option that's water resistant and stain proof. It doesn't require grout, so it's easy to install and has zero maintenance. Vinyl is a long-lasting choice that mimics the look of hardwood, concrete, stone, and tile, but at a lower price point. In sheet form, it is extremely economical and easy to install, while planks and tiles look better and cost more.

CEMENT tiles are popular for graphic flooring styles. They're highly durable and come in a myriad of shapes and colors. However, it's a porous material that requires sealing and can still be prone to staining.

Black and white floors, like this simple ceramic pattern, have long been associated with bathroom decor.

ABOVE: Installed in a herringbone pattern, slate and marble produce very different looks. The low variation in these slate tiles (top) creates an understated flooring compared to the marble's attention-grabbing mix of colors (above). Both are luxurious.

LEFT: The designer of this primary bath chose porcelain tile to cover most of the surfaces in this room. The porcelain tile has a somewhat rugged and stonelike appearance.

These homeowners designed a warm and bright space that blends natural elements in classic and modern styles.

FAR RIGHT: Simple but not plain, the varied textures in this primary bath—from the floor tiles to the cane cabinet accents—are key to the inviting aesthetic.

TOP RIGHT: A wood vanity and quartzite stone countertops anchor the room's focus on natural materials. The brass faucets have a living finish, which shows patina and age with time.

it's in the DETAILS

MIDDLE RIGHT: Natural color variations of clay shine through the fun floor tile. The interlocking star and cross shapes are repeated in the cross handles of the plumbing hardware.

BOTTOM RIGHT: Thin glazed brick wall tile in a stacked formation with matching grout is modern, but the natural texture of bricks adds warmth.

DESIGN BY PLURAL DESIGN STUDIO, CONTRACTOR LIND NELSON CONSTRUCTION, PHOTOGRAPHY AND STYLING BY MALLORY LUNKE.

Chic Countertops

Durability and maintenance are the two key characteristics when it comes to choosing countertop materials. The vanity is home to a lot of bathroom activity, so you want something that can withstand everything that you're throwing at it, whether that's toothpaste, hard water residue, soap, cosmetics, or hot curling irons. Many vanities come with a countertop or a limited selection of countertops, but with custom cabinetry the possibilities are endless.

While walls and floors can be bold and colorful, countertops tend to be neutral and earthy, but that doesn't mean they're boring. Opportunities to incorporate style include countertop thickness, edge details, or extending the countertop's reach with a backsplash. Pattern comes into play with the natural veining and colorways available in stone and stone-look materials, which range from subtle to dramatic.

GO GREEN

Want to make an eco-conscious choice? Look at manufacturing processes. This carbon-neutral quartz product was made using 99% reused water, 100% renewable electric energy, and at least 20% recycled raw materials.

Smart design choices for your countertop can make life easier for you. Minimal patterns and color variations make it easier to see what's on the surface, whether that's standing water, your tweezers, or where a dropped pill landed.

If you need a larger surface, like for cosmetics or hair appliances, choose a vanity with a long countertop and a single sink.

This countertop material is also used as a small backsplash. The countertop is repeated on an adjacent wall, giving the entire vanity area a tailored, high-end look.

Quartz, an engineered stone, and quartzite, a natural stone, are the most popular countertops today. **QUARTZ** is a composite material produced by binding stone chips (typically quartz) to powders and resins to form an extremely durable product. Its textured and variegated look resembles stone, but the patterns formed are more consistent and it's available in more colors. Engineered stone cleans easily and is heat and scratch-resistant. Because it's nonporous, it doesn't need to be sealed or polished for it to resist stains and retain its finish. In most cases, quartz composite prices are comparable to natural stone.

QUARTZITE—like other common **NATURAL STONE**, such as marble, granite, or slate—has a refined look and yet it's extremely durable. Stone is a quality choice for a countertop because of the beauty of its grain and natural colors. Finishes vary from polished to honed, matte, and tumbled. Most stone is porous and therefore must be sealed against etching and staining, meaning countertops like quartzite do require more maintenance than their engineered stone counterparts. No two pieces of stone look alike, so if you prefer uniformity, consider an engineered stone.

A quartz countertop transitions into the shower enclosure with a dramatic waterfall edge. Not only stylish, it also protects the vanity cabinets from water.

This quartz washbasin merges a sink and countertop in one. This design eliminates the hard-to-clean seams and rims that normally result when sinks and countertops come together.

This eye-catching marble countertop creates a stunning and unexpected focal point. The cabinet paint and hardware finish draw their colors from the veining.

SOLID SURFACING is a synthetic material made of polyester or acrylic. It costs almost as much per linear foot as natural stone, but it wears long and well. It's impervious to water, making it a great countertop. Solid-surfacing material comes in many colors, ranging from an assortment of neutrals to intense hues. Some types come with built-in antibacterial protection.

LAMINATE is made of layers of melamine, paper, and plastic resin that are bonded under heat and pressure and then glued to particleboard or plywood. It's available in many colors and textures with a spectrum of pricing, depending on the quality and style you select. It's generally water-resistant and requires no maintenance, but lesser grades will chip and crack. It's not heat resistant, so look out for curling irons and other hot tools. Laminate countertops are relatively easy to install and available as prefabricated units, so it's more DIY friendly than many other materials.

GLASS can also be used to create strikingly beautiful countertops that are easy to clean. These can be solid glass that's either clear or tinted with virtually any color you like (effectively hiding contents of the vanity). Glass can scratch and chip, and it shows water spots and dirt more than a patterned material.

Made of recycled glass chips embedded in pigmented portland cement, terrazzo style countertops add a splash of color and pattern to the vanity. These types of countertops typically require sealing for protection from stains.

TOP: This acrylic countertop was fabricated with an ornate edge that complements the other traditional cabinetry details.

LEFT: The square countertop edge of this glass countertop complements contemporary designs.

BOTTOM: Keep both comfort and style in mind when specifying countertops. The rounded edge on this solid surface countertop is more comfortable than a sleek edge to lean against when looking closely in the vanity mirror.

Tub and Shower Surrounds

In addition to general wall and floor considerations, tubs and showers have some specific surfaces to keep in mind.

Whether a single panel or a full enclosure, glass is the surface of choice for non-recessed shower installations—though even a built-in shower is likely to have a glass shower door. Glass allows light into the shower, while helping the whole room look bigger because you're not visually shortening the room with a closed off space. Glass can be clear or opaque, and the screen or entire enclosure can be gridded, framed, or frameless. Half shower walls topped with glass are also common.

A drop-in tub is installed into a supporting structure. The tub deck—the top of the installation—is essentially a countertop, so you'll be looking for materials that stand up to pooling water. Because water splashes and drips, it's helpful for walls adjacent to the tub, as well as the sides of a built-in structure, to withstand moisture—or at least be easily wiped down without showing signs of condensation.

And don't forget the classic, prefabricated acrylic and fiberglass tub and shower surrounds. These budget-friendly options are easy to install and care for, but you'll sacrifice the style of other shower wall options.

Glass-topped half-walls offer more privacy and they're easier to keep looking clean than an all-glass screen. In this walk-in shower, the wall also houses shower valves so you can turn on water and adjust temperature safely away from the spray.

LEFT: Moisture gathers on the ceiling above a shower, too, so it's not uncommon to find a shower's wall tile running up the ceiling for added protection.

BOTTOM: Even a few inches of tile can provide enough protection for walls around a drop-in tub. Here, the same tile covers the sides of the tub enclosure.

SMART APPROACH: CHOOSING SURFACE MATERIALS

Compare the advantages and disadvantages of materials to determine what works for your home and your lifestyle. Things to consider include:

MAINTENANCE

Okay, so you can afford to splurge on a gorgeous marble vanity top. But are you willing to routinely maintain it and treat it with TLC? If not, easy-care synthetic material is a practical alternative. Your cleaning style and preferences should absolutely influence your selection. Remember grout in your maintenance evaluation, too. Also consider what products are required for cleaning and maintenance. Are you prepared to buy and store anything additional?

LONGEVITY

Do you plan to stay in the house for years, or will you be selling in the near future? How long do you want the materials to last? Consider the long-term. If you're planning to list your house, or your surface can be easily refreshed later without a major remodel, you might feel more comfortable going with a trendy material or color choice. Splurging on the most expensive materials might not be worth it if you'll be moving, but you may see it worthy of a forever home investment. Durable, long-lasting surfaces for a hardworking family bath may be prudent, or you may be saving for a larger remodel in the future—meaning something cheap and easy will do the trick for now.

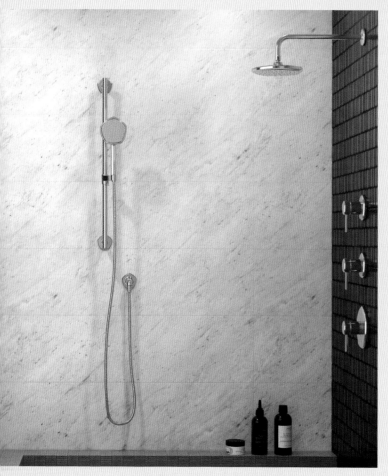

INSTALLATION

Seriously, don't do it yourself if you've chosen an expensive material, such as stone, or one that requires a trained fabricator, such as sintered stone or concrete. Manufacturers often will not honor a warranty if you fail to have their material installed by a qualified person.

Don't forget to consider the cost that installation adds as well. That's why a granite counter you thought was $50 per linear foot could actually cost $70 per linear foot installed.

COST

For many people, this is the deciding factor. In that case, you need to know that natural stone will be expensive, but it usually pays back at resale time. In most cases, a synthetic material is more affordable. Quality also impacts cost. It's easy to find products today that look upscale, but are sold at bargain-basement prices. Be careful, however; there may be a good reason why two seemingly identical materials are priced differently. That's why you should never choose a product based solely on looks. Buy the highest grade you can afford. You might pay more for a well-known brand, but usually, the manufacturer has earned its high reputation and it will honor its warranties

CHAPTER 5

VANITIES AND STORAGE

Think about everything you do at the vanity, like flossing and styling hair, applying makeup, and taking out contacts. A lot of "stuff" is needed for all those grooming, dressing, and pampering activities, as well as cleaning the room itself. A bathroom simply isn't successful without space for those many, varied accouterments. Thankfully, there are plenty of options available, from out-of-the-box additions—like open shelves and robe hooks—to totally custom cabinetry, so you can always make the most of a tiny powder room or a large en suite bath.

When it comes to furnishing your bath, one size does not fit all—choose solutions that meet your space, storage, and style needs.

Practical and Stylish

Vanities are the key source of storage in most baths, but they're often supplemented by additional cabinets, shelving, hooks, or freestanding furniture. The right mix of storage will keep the space feeling composed—not cluttered—while making it easy to see and access the things you use most. With the assortment of bathroom storage options, there's really no excuse for cluttering the tub ledge with shampoo bottles and leaving towels on the floor.

If it's a primary bath, you may want to splurge on upscale cabinetry. The same goes for a powder room; because it's small, you may be able to afford something extra nice—just think about how special your guests will feel! If the cabinetry is for a family bath that will get a lot of wear and tear, choose something that's durable and easy to clean.

Vanities and other storage certainly add style, but more importantly, well-planned storage can improve daily routines and make a better experience for guests. The time to start planning bathroom storage is before you've actually begun the remodeling or building process.

RIGHT: Consider location when selecting storage. Hooks and open shelves make sense to keep linens close at hand for the tub, while vanity drawers can hold extra essentials, like tissues, soap, and hand towels near the toilet and sink.

BOTTOM: A generous-size double vanity makes it possible for two people to get ready for the day at the same time.

Q&A

I don't want to discover too late that I haven't adequately planned storage for my new primary bath. How do I do it?

what the experts say

Designer Susan Obercian says, "Before I start design work for a bathroom, I have my clients answer a two-page questionnaire about their preferences for the new bathroom." This space is very personal, and everyone has their own wishes. That being said, of course, the size of the room will sometimes be the dictating factor for storage options. There is no formula.

People who have never worked with a design professional sometimes feel intimidated by the prospect, usually because they think it will cost too much money. But it's more affordable than you think. Working with a design professional at the outset of a bathroom project can help you avoid a frustrating—and sometimes costly—mistake.

what real people do

For a modest, sometimes hourly, fee, a professional can offer ideas and options you wouldn't know about otherwise. Check out designers and firms that offer e-design services. But even without a design pro, you can take some of the same steps suggested by Obercian. Start off by making a list of who will use the bathroom. Consider their routines and list what they use and will need to keep in the room. Add on additional things that will need storage, like clean towels, extra tissues, or cleaning supplies. Then think about where those items will be stored, aiming to keep similar items together, such as all bath towels on one shelf. Keep bathroom cleaners separate from other items when possible, and also plan for safe storage for medications.

Sometimes, it's simply a matter of making choices with the most storage potential, even without a detailed plan. Choosing a freestanding vanity over a wall-mount vanity, for example, will give you more storage. Locating a vanity on a wall, instead of at a window, will leave room for medicine cabinets above the sink. When budget allows, custom cabinetry will maximize the space you have.

Planning storage and vanity needs is an important part of the remodeling and building processes. This custom bath was a collaboration between the homeowner and a design professional.

This bath packs storage into vertical space above the tub and between console sinks. The console only has a few small drawers, so keeping towels in the built-in is handy for both the lav and the bath.

Vanities

Choosing a vanity cabinet deserves as much consideration as selecting cabinetry for a new kitchen. Not only does the vanity provide critical storage and a work surface, but it also helps anchor the style of the room.

There are two standard vanity types:

FLOATING vanities are affixed to the wall, leaving an open area underneath. Also called wall-mount vanities, they're typical in more contemporary bath designs and are commonly used in small spaces, too. They also offer the most installation flexibility, as the fixture can be hung at whatever height is most comfortable for the user. **FLOOR-MOUNT** vanities rest on the floor and are often called freestanding vanities. Though standard in more traditional design styles, these furniture-like vanities offer more design flexibility and often more storage, too.

Another term you may encounter are **BUILT-IN** vanities. Like kitchen cabinets, these are customized to fit into the architecture of the room, often between walls and into corners. They can be wall-mounted or freestanding, but are typically flush to the wall.

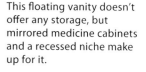

This floating vanity doesn't offer any storage, but mirrored medicine cabinets and a recessed niche make up for it.

Built into an alcove, this custom double vanity includes details that match the architecture and millwork in the room.

This freestanding vanity is actually a repurposed antique dry sink. Because the top requires only small holes for plumbing, the conversion didn't compromise the piece's structural integrity.

A console sink is something of a hybrid, mounting both to the wall and the floor. It's a great solution for small spaces or rooms with eye-catching wallcoverings to show off. Though it doesn't have storage, it does have a roomy countertop.

Vanities are available three ways:

- **STOCK.** Factory-made in a range of standard heights, sizes, and finishes, stock vanities are usually, but not always, the most economical type. Styles are more limited.
- **SEMI-CUSTOM.** Factory-made with customized options upon your order, semi-custom vanities are usually midrange in price. Your customizations may include size, finish, base style, countertop, sink and faucet installation type, and hardware. They also may offer extras such as pullout bins, spinout trays, special door styles, drawer organizers, and custom finishes.
- **CUSTOM.** Built-to-order to your bathroom's specifications, custom vanity cabinets can be designed by your architect, interior designer, or designer/builder. Everything from the size, door styles, color, and interior accessories can be tailored to your specifications. This is typically the most expensive option.

Vanities may be sold as an entire package—cabinet, countertop, and even sink and faucet—or sold as cabinet base only, letting you select everything, from countertop to hardware. Of course, there are options in between, too. A custom vanity built to fit the room and your needs is one way to go, or you can purchase a wallet-friendly stock vanity that can be quickly selected and installed.

A vanity's details can be integral to the room's aesthetic. In this bath, the green stone countertop coordinates with the penny round floor tile accents.

TOP: Custom cabinetry—and some semi-custom models—allow you to specify specialized interior storage like these compartmentalized drawers.

LEFT: Custom cabinetry includes offering upper storage, like this medicine cabinet, tailored to the vanity and the space.

Here, vibrant panels accent cabinet doors—the shades of green are also found in the flooring and wall accent tiles.

Standard widths for stock and semi-custom vanities range from 24, 30, 36, 48, 60, and 72 inches, but you'll find plenty of in-between sizes, too. Standard depth is 20–21 inches, though they can be as slim as 18 inches and as deep as 24 inches. Shallow vanities free up floor space, and they're more accessible than deep vanities for children or people who are seated when using the vanity. Deeper models store more. If you're using custom or semi-custom cabinetry to create your own vanity, you'll be looking at similar depth options, but building your own widths by pairing sink and drawer bases, hamper bases, and linen cabinets.

Vanities offer a variety of storage options, from clutter-hiding doors and drawers to open shelves and wide countertops. Some vanities offer little in the way of storage, but pack a punch when it comes to design (these are great for powder rooms). What you get will depend on how you use the bath, the size and shape of the space, your budget, and the style you're trying to achieve.

The vanity may be the star of the bath, or blend with the room to let other elements stand out. A thick acrylic countertop resembles glass and creates a dramatic juxtaposition with the textured pebble wall accented by downlighting.

With exposed hinges and ribbed glass, this apothecary-inspired vanity has a nostalgic style that's further enhanced by the classic tilting vanity mirror and shaded sconces. It's perfectly complemented by the ceramic tiled walls that cover the bath.

Contrasting wall coverings and vanity finishes draws attention. Using the contrasting color in other elements, such as lighting or plumbing fixtures, will keep it from looking out of place.

This spacious bath combines furniture and built-in storage for a stylish, clutter-free haven.

FAR RIGHT: Flanking a window and freestanding tub, double vanities provide separate grooming areas for two. Almost unseen, recessed wall cabinets at each vanity provide even more storage.

it's in the DETAILS

TOP RIGHT: Recessed shelves and towel hooks next to the shower offer plenty of accessible storage. The chaise is a luxurious addition continuing the soft curves also found in the tub and chandelier.

BOTTOM RIGHT: Built-in cabinets with mirrored doors are stylish storage for anything from linens to clothing. The molding and cross panels are a traditional touch, while the mirrored surface ups the glam factor.

Medicine Cabinets

Electrical outlets, USB connections, defoggers, and Bluetooth are some of the techy features accompanying built-in lighting, swing-out mirrors, and storage options in today's medicine cabinets. In addition, some units come with a lock or a separate compartment to securely and safely store potentially dangerous substances. Medicine cabinets can be wall-mounted or recessed. Wall-mounted versions protrude off the wall, so depending on the size, they can make a small space feel cramped and might conflict with some vanity lighting.

4. LADDERS

7. SHOWER NICHES

TOP 10
Storage Ideas That Aren't Cabinetry

Whether you're looking for new ideas or simply don't have space for another big piece of furniture, here's what's tried, true, and trending in storage.

2. HOOKS

1. Heated towel bars are a place to hang in-use towels while offering a bit of luxury, too.

2. Hooks give guests a place to not only dry their towels, but also a way to keep clothes and toiletries off the floor or countertop when space is limited.

3. Baskets keep things like towels or laundry out of sight, and can easily be moved when needed. Smaller baskets and trays decoratively corral items on countertops and shelving.

4. Ladders can dry and store towels, hang robes, and provide storage for soaps and other bath necessities—all with a limited impact on floorspace.

5. Wall shelves are an easy way to add readily accessible storage to a blank wall, regardless of the size of the room.

6. Linen closets built into walls, even shallow ones, will effectively hide clutter. Deeper models are ideal for storing towels.

7. Shower niches prevent the need for hanging caddies and other unsecure shower storage.

8. Tub surrounds can be customized to conceal tilt-open or pull-out storage in the base.

9. Coat racks provide vertical storage perfect for bathrobes and keeping clothes off the floor.

10. Outdoor accent stools withstand moisture and can easily be moved around where needed, like next to a tub for a convenient surface away from the splash zone.

Bathroom Furniture

Spacious bathrooms, especially primary baths, can be furnished like other rooms in the house—armoires and dressers, dressing tables, and even upholstered seating may be part of the plan. In addition, fine-furniture details, like door panel inserts or shapely feet, have upped the style quotient of even the most modest stock cabinets.

With sustainability and craftsmanship in equal demand, incorporating vintage and repurposed furniture is a big part of home design right now. In the bath, it's a chance to create personalized storage—and style—solutions by mixing built-in cabinetry with freestanding pieces like bookshelves, consoles, DIY shelving, or apothecary-style cabinets.

An antique dresser makes a unique vanity.

GET SMART

Most furniture finishes will hold up fine in the bathroom, as long as they're not subjected to standing water. If you're converting a piece for a vanity, replace the top with impervious material like stone, tile, or quartz, or cover the top with glass or coat it with polyurethane or marine varnish.

TOP LEFT: A built-in armoire serves several purposes, including linen storage. Behind one of the doors, there's an ironing center; the board drops down when the door is open. A pull-out hamper hides in another.

TOP RIGHT: A built-in dresser makes practical use of a small nook at one end of this primary bath.

BOTTOM LEFT: Furniture elements come together for a chic dressing table area.

Unfitted furniture, including a freestanding vanity, allow the tiles and wallpaper to stand out in this transitional bath.

FAR RIGHT: A slim console table provides storage and countertop space without impeding too much on the floor plan. The decorative stool can move around the room to offer seating, or a place for reading materials to stay dry while you soak in the tub.

it's in the DETAILS

TOP RIGHT: A thin-profile wall-mount mirror sits closely against the wall allowing an elegantly high-arched faucet at the sink.

MIDDLE AND BOTTOM RIGHT: A mix of hooks and bars keep items conveniently at hand, and can be installed for the best height for the users.

Linens and Things

A linen closet—in the bath or right outside—provides excellent space for towels and other bulky items, like hot rollers, heating pads, or extra toilet paper rolls and tissue boxes. If a full-size linen closet is out of the question, there are plenty of alternatives: add a tall linen cupboard to a vanity, or make use of the space in the wall between two studs for recessed shelving.

Open shelving is another option that works for everything from towels to toiletries, art, and greenery. Whether hung on the wall, recessed between the studs, or given a built-in look, it's versatile and easy to incorporate even in limited space. A major benefit of open storage is that it's often the most accessible and makes it easy to find things, especially for guests in your home. Another benefit is that open shelving offers storage without visually closing off the room. But it's a balancing act—untamed visible storage can make a room look and feel cluttered. Things like cleaning supplies and personal items are better hidden behind doors; towels, soaps, cotton balls, loofahs, and other smaller items corralled in canisters, boxes, and baskets can be decoratively stored.

This double vanity fits between walls under a sloping ceiling. The open shelving below stores extra towels, which also add a bit of color to the room.

When space allows, why not add purely decorative elements? It elevates the style of the space and puts it on par with the other rooms in the home that are thoughtfully decorated.

A built-in cabinet uses vertical space for linens and a hamper.

Beautiful mahogany-stained cabinets transformed what was once a nondescript bath in an older house into a showplace.

FAR RIGHT: Custom vanities built into opposite corners make the most of the space. Joining them is a large dresser-like cabinet with drawers and shelves for storing bath towels and other linens.

it's in the DETAILS

TOP RIGHT: You can see how neatly the cabinet fits into the corner. The vessel lav resembles a bowl sitting on top of the counter.

BOTTOM RIGHT: The position of the vanity left room for a heated towel rack next to the shower.

SMART APPROACH: GETTING ORGANIZED

1. DETERMINE WHAT YOU NEED

Start by identifying a space you want to organize, like the linen closet, under the sink, or inside vanity drawers. Remove everything currently stored, including any removable organizers. Get rid of things that are broken, expired, or you no longer use. Then, group like things that you'll want to store together, like cleaning supplies, towels, cosmetics, and medicine.

It's recommended to tackle one area at a time, rather than starting too large of an organization project. But if storage in the bathroom overall isn't working, you're free to try rethinking the entire room—just be sure to allow yourself plenty of time, and lots of space for sorting, to complete the project.

2. MEASURE AND OUTFIT THE STORAGE SPACE

Measure the storage space (height, width, and depth). Also note the sizes of items you're planning to store. With that understanding of space and items, you can adequately plan and purchase organizers. Look for storage solutions that will keep clutter corralled and make it easier to find and access what you need. Stackable slide-out drawers or shelves maximize open space under the sink. Lazy Susans make it easy to find items that are stored in the back of the cabinet. Racks for items, like hairbrushes, curling irons, and bulky blow dryers, mount to the inside of cabinet doors. Baskets look great on open shelving.

No matter how fun it is to pick out baskets, bins, and other organizers, refrain from buying those items until you know both what you need to store and the size of the space where you'll be storing them.

CHAPTER 6

LIGHT AND AIR

Good lighting and healthy air circulation are important factors in your bath's design. Light, ventilation, and heating work together to rid the bath of odors and moisture, creating a safe space perfect for starting your day, looking your best, and welcoming guests. Air quality and lighting considerations aren't difficult to understand, and following expert advice won't cost you a fortune. Here's what you need to know to make your space gorgeous and comfortable.

From stylish sconces to quiet fans and luxuriously heated floors, it's easier than ever to get a more efficient and enjoyable bath. The perfect combination of these key elements will keep your bath beautiful, safe, and healthy for years to come.

Natural Light

The best complement to your bathroom is the most natural: daylight. Not only does the room look better when it's bathed with warm, natural light, but it makes you look better, too. If privacy allows, a large window or a bank of windows will add to the luxuriousness of a bathroom. For those who want to bring in light but desire more privacy, there are multiple solutions. Small windows high on the wall, like transom windows, work well in many baths. When you can't add a window, a vented skylight may be an option.

If you want natural light to be part of your bathing ritual, consider the direction of the window in terms of the sun. Early morning sun comes from the east; late afternoon sun comes from the west. If your window faces south, your bathroom will get direct sunlight most of the day; if the window faces north, it won't get much direct sunlight at all.

RIGHT: Large picture windows feel sleek and contemporary, and contribute to a lavish bathing experience, too.

Casement windows with grilles open out to the side and are compatible with traditional architecture.

You don't have to sacrifice wall space with high-set windows that offer natural light and plenty of privacy.

GET SMART

Greatly enhanced glazing options and low-E (low-emissivity) glass have solved the problem of drafty, inefficient windows—and the lost energy dollars associated with them.

Thoughtful design can make a modest sized bath perform as though it is much larger. It will feel larger, too, thanks to simple material choices that brighten the space.

FAR RIGHT: On one end of the layout, a half-wall and glass partition section off the bath and shower while admitting natural light into the entire room.

it's in the
DETAILS

TOP RIGHT: A pocket door closes off the water closet and takes up no floor space. The frosted glass panel allows additional light into the separate space.

BOTTOM RIGHT: There's plenty of room for grooming, and adequate storage at the double vanity. A beautiful and smart decor choice, wide beveled mirrors look polished and reflect ambient light.

Artificial Light

Artificial lighting is an important component of a well-lit bath, even in rooms with plenty of natural light. It's imperative when dark outside, as well as in baths without windows. Lighting should be layered. You will need adequate **AMBIENT**, or general, lighting for overall illumination and suitable **TASK LIGHTING** for grooming, reading labels, or other activities. **ACCENT LIGHTING** adds illumination to dark areas, like cabinet interiors, and can be used to highlight an interesting detail, such as a tray ceiling. For your senses, consider **DECORATIVE LIGHTING**, which enhances lighting overall, but is mostly ornamental.

RIGHT: Though not always possible, it's ideal to position vanity lighting on both sides of the mirror.

LEFT: A light fixture that casts light up, rather than down, can help avoid countertop glare.

The right lighting lets you use dark and moody finishes without the space feeling gloomy and dim.

GET SMART

When it comes to lighting, sustainability is easy to prioritize. LED lighting uses less energy than other forms and is the most common lighting solution.

Illuminating Ideas

Use a combination of windows and light fixtures when possible. Ambient natural light is energy efficient and natural, while artificial light will almost always offer the best task and accent lighting.

Consider custom applications of LED lighting to highlight architectural features and promote better safety. Here, it not only provides a night-light along the floor, but LED lighting is also built into the cabinetry flanking the mirror.

4. SKYLIGHTS

6. FIXTURES WITH ADDED LIGHT

TOP 10
Ways to Maximize Lighting

8. GLASS BLOCK

1. Light colors on surfaces, like walls, flooring, countertops, and even vanities, will help a small room feel brighter. Dark stone and highly textured surfaces can trap light according to the NKBA.

2. White ceilings effectively distribute ambient light. For example, it helps pull natural light from one window into the rest of the room.

3. Reflective surfaces—like mirrors or glossy finishes on cabinets or wall tiles—help disperse light. The NKBA cautions against glaring reflections on surfaces like highly polished countertops.

4. Skylights add natural light without requiring wall space. They provide about five times as much light as a comparable wall window, according to the NKBA. An operable skylight can provide ventilation, too, and some of these units work by remote control for easy operation.

5. A solar tunnel, which could be described as a tubular skylight, makes it possible to bring natural light into any room, even a lower floor in a multi-level house.

6. Fixtures with added lighting such as mirrors, vent fans, and even toilets can be an additional, uncommon source for light.

7. LED strip lighting fits where traditional lights don't, adding light under shelves, along the floor, and other impactful spots.

8. Glass block provides both privacy and light. It's one example of what's called a "fixed window," which means you can't open it.

9. Interior glass panels, like glass shower walls or glass-paneled pocket doors, allow more light to disseminate in the space—even if the glass is frosted for privacy.

10. Dimmers are a little luxury that can help the space transition from hardworking to relaxing. They're also great for lighting during late-night trips to the bathroom.

Attractive Fixtures

Light fixtures put the finishing touch on your bath. You can find anything from sculptural ceiling lights to sleek cylindrical sconces. Besides style, finish should play a role in your choice. Although it's generally recommended to match finishes and styles between plumbing fixtures, anything goes with lighting. Choosing a style and finish that's compatible with the other elements in the room feels consistent and integrated, while variation will make lighting choices stand out.

RIGHT: Elegant lighting adds interest in a mostly monochromatic bath. The playful shapes in this bath catch your eye and complement the lively color.

Opal and opaque glass shades soften light and provide a warm glow.

Q&A

What type of lighting should I use at the vanity so I can look my best?

what the experts say

From applying makeup to shaving, lighting is an important part of the grooming center. Bathroom lighting should illuminate both sides of the face, under the chin, and the top of the head. Combine side sconces with a fixture above the mirror for the best cross-illumination, which avoids shadows from using downlighting alone. Ideally, these sidelights would be installed to take into account the user's height to reduce glare and maximize lighting the face. Lights would also not have clear glass and exposed bulbs, but utilize opaque glass to reduce glare and soften lighting. Fixtures should be damp rated, meaning they can withstand moist environments and locations.

what real people do

A bathroom that's very small may only have one light source. If that's the case, the light source should be at the mirror—ideally side fixtures that can serve as task lights and general illumination. It's not a good idea to use a ceiling fixture alone because, although it can provide adequate ambient light, it can't offer the type of light that you need to apply makeup or shave at the mirror. If you can only use a light fixture above the mirror, the NKBA recommends using the longest one that will fit in the space. A freestanding lighted magnifying or makeup mirror may be needed to supplement lighting for some tasks.

An easy way to ensure good, all-around lighting at a vanity is to purchase a mirror with LED lights incorporated into it. This model is also dimmable. Here, it complements task lighting at the double vanity.

COLOR TEMPERATURE

Lighting color temperature is measured in Kelvins and ranges from warm to cool. Warm lighting, which is more yellow in color, is about 3000K or lower. Cool lighting is bluer in color and measures 4000K and above. Generally, warm light akin to daylight is the preferred temperature for the vanity area. Light bulbs will have a color temperature measurement. In addition, there are LED light bulbs and lighted fixtures that can change from warm to cool, so you can pick the best for you and your space.

Layering sources of light adds style and increases functionality in any size bath. This space from Golden Rule Builders uses light-enhancing surface features, too.

FAR RIGHT: Two windows are the source of natural light, while a chandelier, recessed ceiling lights, and vanity lights provide overall and task-oriented lighting.

TOP RIGHT: A window above the built-in tub allows privacy—with a view—while bathing. Glass above this partial wall lets the light brighten the dark corner of the shower as well.

it's in the DETAILS

MIDDLE RIGHT: The separate toilet includes recessed ceiling light, but a pass-through window provides access to natural light during the day.

BOTTOM RIGHT: The toilet includes a night-light type feature, too.

DESIGN BY GOLDEN RULE BUILDERS, PHOTOGRAPHY BY KAAN OZTURK.

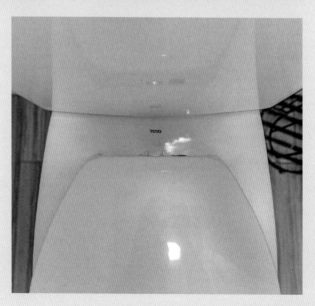

Lighting Tubs and Showers

Light around the tub and shower area must be bright enough for safety and grooming. You want lighting that's comfortable for tasks, like shaving or reading shampoo bottles. Good lighting will also help when it comes to cleaning these areas, too. According to the NKBA, a shower with translucent glass or a shower curtain may not require a separate light if the room has strong ambient lighting. However, if a shower enclosure is more than 10 square feet, it should have a separate light inside.

Any light fixture installed in a wet or damp area must be designed for such use; look for damp and/or wet rated light fixtures. Though not every area in the bath is close to water, fixtures still may benefit from being damp rated. Your electrician will know how to handle installation requirements and can also recommend proper fixtures for your space.

All the light sources in this space contribute to lighting the tub area.

TOP: Another way to brighten a tub/shower area is with an operable skylight, which also provides ventilation.

BOTTOM: Whether you're taking a quick shower or a long soak, you need good lighting.

SMART APPROACH: PLAN YOUR LIGHTING

LAY IT OUT

Place your general lighting first, and then indicate where you'll need task lights (a good place to start is around the mirror). Where are you doing activities that require light, such as applying makeup, putting in contacts, or reading labels? Don't forget the benefit of light in a shower for things like shaving or cleaning grout. When the hardworking lighting is planned, look for opportunities to add accent and decorative lighting, which can indirectly light the room and highlight its best features. Also consider where you might like accent lighting to brighten dark spots, like inside linen closets and cabinet interiors.

GET CONTROL

In addition to where your lighting will be located, think about how you'll turn it on. You won't want all light fixtures turned off and on by the same light switch, because all lighting won't always be needed. Light switches, as well as ventilation switches, dimmers, and other bathroom controls, should be 36–48 inches above the floor so that most people, standing or seated, can reach them. In addition to traditional flip (rocker) light switches, look for hands-free or motion sensing fixtures. These not only prevent accidentally leaving lights on, but can also help those with accessibility issues get a safely lit space without a struggle.

Try making a rough sketch of your bathroom's layout, then indicating where various light fixtures will be. This can help you identify areas that may be left in the dark, as well as spots where you'll want access to lighting controls.

Decorative lighting adds drama and function to this space.

Clear the Air

Adequate ventilation is a must for your bathroom. It not only whisks away odor, but it also combats the steam and condensation that cause mildew, rot, and deterioration of the bathroom's surfaces, possibly even exterior and interior walls. If you haven't installed a proper vapor barrier between the bathroom and the exterior wall, you may face serious structural damage in addition to peeling and chipping paint.

The simplest form of ventilation is natural: a window. If you don't have access to a traditional window, consider a vented skylight or a roof window. Most local building codes require fans in bathrooms that don't have windows. Even if you have access to natural ventilation, there are certain times you won't want to keep a window open (the middle of winter, for example).

Fans and windows can be used to target certain areas, such as the shower, to help more quickly and effectively remove moisture. And don't overlook powder rooms—they might lack the moisture of a full bath, but they benefit from air circulation, too.

BOTTOM LEFT: Hot air rises, and windows opened at the top make good sense.

BOTTOM RIGHT: Windows in the shower not only offer natural light, but an escape for air and moisture, too.

Many showers are open at the top to allow ventilation, but steam-enhanced showers have to be tightly enclosed while in use. A transom above the shower door flips open to help to clear the air after use, and a vent fan is installed close by.

Ventilation Systems

Fan-based ventilation benefits every bath, even those with plenty of windows. There are three main types of bathroom ventilation systems available for your consideration.

A **RECIRCULATING FAN** pulls air through a charcoal filter and then returns it to the room, rather than venting it to the outside. Its big advantage is that it requires no ducting. However, the charcoal filter only removes odors, not moisture, from the air. This type of fan might do the job for a powder room where there's little moisture to exhaust, but it's not a good choice for a room with a shower.

SURFACE-MOUNTED DUCTED FANS consist of a fan unit that gets mounted in the wall or ceiling and exhausts the air through ductwork. Ceiling models are often combined with a light fixture.

IN-LINE FANS are mounted in the ductwork rather than on a wall or ceiling. As a result, one of these fans can exhaust air from multiple bathrooms or from two or more locations in a large bathroom.

GET SMART

Bath fans are imperative for fighting moisture damage, but they're easily forgotten and often turned off too early even when they're used. Upgrade to a humidity sensing fan, which runs automatically when moisture is detected and shuts off when no longer needed.

CHOOSE THE RIGHT EXHAUST FAN

To remove moist air and odors effectively, match the fan's capacity to the room's volume. Ventilating fans are sized by the number of cubic feet of air they move each minute (cubic feet per minute, or CFM).

Fans are also rated in "sones" for the amount of noise they produce. A fan rated at 1 sone is the quietest. Investing in a quiet, right-sized model makes the space more enjoyable for everyone.

BATHROOM SIZE	MINIMUM VENTILATION (CFM) REQUIRED
Less than 50 sq. ft.	50 CFM
50–100 sq. ft.	1 CFM per sq. ft. of floor space
More than 100 sq. ft.	"Add the CFM requirement for each fixture: Toilet 50 CFM Shower 50 CFM Bathtub 50 CFM Jetted tub 100 CFM"
Separate toilet or shower area enclosed by door	Install an additional fan for the size of the enclosed space

Even a bathroom with a window needs a fan. In a larger bath, if you have the option, install the ventilation closer to the shower or tub where it can tackle moisture as it rises.

Keeping It Toasty

Smart design features and luxury add-ons can help create a more comfortable atmosphere in your bath.

RADIANT-FLOOR HEAT, for example, is energy efficient, invisible, and space saving (no radiators or baseboard heaters). The increasingly popular system uses hot water or electric wire coils installed underneath the floor. As the floor warms up, heat rises to take the chill out of the rest of the room, as well. Typically, radiant heat is a viable option only if you're replacing a floor or building from scratch.

TOE-KICK HEATERS fit neatly into dead space under a vanity cabinet. These electric heat sources provide a pleasant blast of warm air on demand with just the flip of a switch. Similarly, heating ducts in walls and floors can be rerouted to the toe-kick area. A warmed floor at the sink or vanity is particularly welcome by bare feet in colder weather—even more so when paired with naturally cool flooring materials like stone and ceramic.

Imagine wrapping yourself in a toasty towel to ease the transition out of a steamy shower. **TOWEL WARMERS** are becoming standard fare in bath design, particularly in primary suites. There are two types. Hydronic models are essentially pipes that are hooked up to hot water from radiators or radiant floors. The other type uses electricity. In small spaces, these fixtures can also be a source of ambient heat.

Or, step out of the shower and into a warming glow. Using infrared bulbs that radiate heat into the space, **HEAT LAMPS** are usually mounted in the ceiling around the tub or outside the shower area. Similarly, a **CONVECTION HEATER** can be engaged to warm and circulate the air using a small fan that is built into the device. Some come with exhaust fans and lights.

RIGHT: A fireplace insert is a simple luxury that adds ambiance and warms the air for an extra cozy soak in the tub.

LEFT: A heated towel bar is another feature that homeowners are incorporating into their bath for added pampering. They can be mounted to the wall or installed to stand alone, like the one pictured here.

CHAPTER 7

ADDING STYLE

Defining your style is perhaps the most fun phase of your project. Remember, today's bathroom is more than utilitarian—in fact, it can be a showcase. If you're not sure about what you like or you're at a loss as to how to pull it off, here's some advice about how to create a cohesive look, and a review of some of the common elements in today's most popular styles.

Throw out the rule book and express yourself in colors and designs that you love.

A Chic Retreat

A bathroom can be one of the chicest rooms in a house. In fact, a beautiful bath—whatever its size—is an important selling feature. But when you're renovating or building a bath for yourself, you should strive to give it a style that speaks to you.

You may want to consult with an interior designer or certified bath designer during this phase of your project. They can guide you and help you choose everything from an overall look and color scheme to window treatments and other decorative details. But don't be afraid to go it alone. Decorating is really about individual taste and choices.

Today, design styles are more fluid than in the past. Instead of following strict decorating rules to achieve a textbook style, the National Kitchen and Bath Association says more spaces are combining multiple design elements to create the perfect personal style. The following pages highlight some of the most popular designs now, but they're certainly not the only looks around.

An antique, stained glass window decorates the open shower and bath area. Stone walls and flooring add to the old world charm.

Look at the home's architecture for style inspiration. Is it modern or traditional? Even if the architecture is nondescript, you can introduce a style-specific look the same way you decorate the other rooms in your home: color, pattern, texture, and certainly, small details that add personality.

A graphic wallpaper proclaims this bath's coastal style.

2. FAUCET SPOUTS AND HANDLES

TOP 10
Places to Add Style

Refreshing a current bath or
creating a whole new space, these
small details are big opportunities
for personal style.

1. CABINETRY HARDWARE

6. WALL ART

4. LIGHT FIXTURES

3. MIRRORS

1. Cabinetry hardware can be the jewelry of your vanity, and they're a quick way to give a new look to an old vanity.

2. Faucet spouts and handles reflect your bath's style. They run the gamut from sleek and simple to elegant and adorned with crystal or shapely flourishes.

3. Mirrors naturally attract attention, so frame your face with something wow-worthy.

4. Light fixtures are a functional necessity that can pack a punch, whether mounted on the wall or ceiling.

5. Fabrics like window treatments, rugs, shower curtains, and even towels are often simple and neutral elements, but in the right space, they can be used to stand out.

6. Wall art is easily overlooked in the bath, but adds character just like any other room in the home. Plus, it can be easily updated when styles change.

7. Cabinet legs and feet elevate the vanity physically and aesthetically, from traditional turned wood to modern metal lifts.

8. Ceiling details like beams, panels, and coffers make even a little-used secondary bathroom feel special.

9. Shower drains are available in stylish and funky patterns—a fun, unexpected touch to delight guests.

10. Doorknobs are practical, but they can add historic and style-specific details in an often overlooked spot.

Traditional Looks

Traditional style has elements of English and American 18th- and early 19th-century design. The look is rich and formal with architectural elements, such as graceful arches, columns, trimwork, and double-hung windows with muntins or any divided-light window.

Traditional spaces are often outfitted with furniture-like storage and custom cabinetry that fills the space. To create the look, select wood cabinetry finished in a mellow wood stain or painted white with fine details, such as fluted panels, bull's-eye corner blocks, and dentil and crown molding. The cabinet's door style is often a raised-panel design. Hardware that evokes the mood of the period will add the right touch.

Marble is a classic choice for surfaces, although some people prefer granite for the countertop. Wall treatments include molding, wainscotting, and wallpapers in classic prints and patterns. From pleated draperies to upholstered seating, richly patterned, colored, and textured textiles are luxe accents.

Though neutrals are often the foundation, traditional baths aren't afraid to incorporate saturated colors.

TOP: Formal architectural features and millwork are hallmarks of traditional style. Sconces and wallpaper enhance the look.

LEFT: A gracefully shaped backsplash is a subtle detail—it can make a simple stock cabinet worthy of the most traditional decor.

Elegant details make this sophisticated space a modern-day classic.

FAR RIGHT: A beveled mirror, fluted opaque sconces, and raised panel doors have the rich details expected of a traditional bath. Swans and water lilies float on a colorful but still subdued wallpaper. The sophisticated look brings the traditional style into today.

it's in the DETAILS

TOP RIGHT: Above the tub, a roman shade and chandelier bring new patterns and finishes, without competing with the rest of the room. Layered crown molding reflects the details of the vanity's raised-panel cabinetry.

BOTTOM RIGHT: The tub deck and brick backsplash topped with a chair rail trim is a reinterpretation of the vanity's countertop and simple backsplash. Matching widespread faucets in a nickel finish further synchronize the tub and vanity areas.

Trendy Transitional

Once mostly considered an updated version of traditional, transitional style is the most popular look today because of its versatility. Transitional baths combine traditional and modern styles for a look that's simple and relaxed—not quite as formal nor too minimalist. Transitional aims to be balanced, but is easily (and often) skewed one direction. Given today's penchant for mixing styles, it can also incorporate small elements of other styles. But don't take it too far: to stay transitional, it shouldn't be rustic, cluttered, fussy, or cold. If you're a middle-of-the-road type when it comes to decorating, blending elements of the past with those of today is your style.

Color palettes are largely neutral, with softer and more muted shades that are accented with a darker hue. In fact, transitional style gets a lot of its personality from contrasts, like ornate fixtures in a simple shower, a clawfoot tub and sleek cabinets, or a traditional vanity with an abstract mirror. Although clean lines dominate, curves are a welcome variance. Black and brass finishes are popular, as are wood and light stone (or stone-look) materials. Modern lighting works well. Pattern can be incorporated through a fun wallpaper or bold flooring, but it's usually a larger-scale and more contemporary graphic than traditional small florals, for example.

Dark and light, matte and glossy, and rounded and straight elements balance harmoniously in this bath that pairs a vintage clawfoot tub with a modern grooming area.

Traditional pieces like the shaded sconces, cabinetry feet, and arched niches are more subdued without ornate millwork and cabinetry details. Marble tiles in multiple shades create a striking floor pattern; the crisp lines are subtly repeated in the inset cabinet doors and linear pulls.

Ornately traditional brass plumbing fixtures stand out against sleek walls and flooring. The boldly framed shower screen is a starkly contemporary element.

A harmonious mix of repeating contemporary lines and traditional materials create a tailored and welcoming space.

FAR RIGHT: Instead of a plain glass shower enclosure, these gridded panels offer a graphic contrast to the room's light color palette and the traditional stone shower walls.

TOP RIGHT: A traditionally patterned rug draws attention as you enter the room. It softens the tile floor and visually balances the attention-seeking shower screen. The stunning freestanding tub is an example

it's in the
DETAILS

of transitional design all on its own: it has a strong rectangular shape softened with curved sides. The curved and rounded plumbing fixtures are modernized with trendy, warm golden finishes.

BOTTOM RIGHT: Blush pink walls carry the color from the rug into the rest of the room. The subtle color warms up the cool whites, grays, and blacks dominant in the room. The vanity mirror mimics the edges of the shower screen, and the dark countertop helps anchor the dark hue in the room.

DESIGN BY MEL BEAN INTERIORS, PHOTOGRAPHY BY KACEY GILPIN.

Feeling Nostalgic

Call it cottage or Victorian, this look recalls the turn of the last century with a bit of a modern twist. It's certainly much less formal and a lot less cluttered than its inspiration, but it still strikes a nostalgic vibe.

A reproduction tub (often a clawfoot model), a pedestal sink, and matching fittings set the tone. Cabinets are painted, usually white. The door style is typically flat panel—a simpler version of the type of door you'd expect in a traditional-style room—and drawer and door hardware may be simple reproduction knobs in glass, porcelain, or metal. For the walls, white subway tiles and painted paneling like wainscoting, shiplap, or beadboard can pull the style together. On the floor, small tiles like hexagons, squares, or basketweaves evoke the era. If you prefer something warmer underfoot, use wood or a vinyl look-alike. Antique wood furniture would be well-purposed in these spaces.

A bit more rustic and a smidge simpler, farmhouse style is a cousin of these sweet looks. Their aesthetics share many similar elements, though barn doors and exposed beams are common here. Farmhouse today often embraces more modern styling, like black lighting and plumbing finishes and round mirrors, to keep the look from feeling too cutesy.

FAR LEFT: Shades of white and brown are the dominant colors in these spaces, though walls can incorporate softer blues, greens, and yellows.

LEFT: A reproduction tub with a "telephone faucet," and white-painted paneled walls create a pleasantly nostalgic look in this room.

TOP: A steam shower is a modern centerpiece that fits comfortably in this farmhouse space. The bronze frame complements the plumbing, light fixture, and curtain rod, as well as the many wood tones.

This pretty room opens to a private garden and is flooded with light all day.

FAR RIGHT: A pair of pedestal sinks with cross-handle faucets and the hexagon floor tiles are signature vintage selections. Mirrored, built-in medicine cabinets offer storage in lieu of vanity cabinets.

TOP RIGHT: The beadboard wainscot is another period detail. White paint unites the beadboard and the horizontal wide plank paneling on the upper walls and ceiling.

it's in the DETAILS

BOTTOM RIGHT: A beautiful clawfoot tub—an exact reproduction of a turn-of-the-last-century model—is the room's centerpiece. A long soak offers garden views.

In a Modern Mood

You may often see the words "modern" and "contemporary" used interchangeably. But to be precise, they are different styles—though they each have an emphasis on simplicity. If you like a minimum of ornamentation, these looks will appeal to you.

Influenced by German Bauhaus and Scandinavian design, modern style has roots in the early to mid-twentieth century. It uses warm, earthy neutrals with only subtle color. Natural materials are prominently featured. Contemporary actually refers to style that is *of the moment*, which makes it difficult to clearly identify, since it changes over time. Contemporary style is colder, stark, and dramatic, with more contrast than modern design.

Though technically different, they have many similarities. The architecture is spare and right-angled—no decorative trim or arches. Cabinets without a face frame and with flat-panel doors and drawers fill the bill. Hardware and plumbing fixtures are sleek and unobtrusive. Casement or awning windows without grilles are compatible with a modern interior, and window treatments are minimal, if at all.

A bold marble-like pattern is installed in large slabs on the walls and around the tub for an ultra-sleek appearance in this contemporary space. Though also neutral, the fixtures, thick window frames, and mirror appear to pop against the room's swirling backdrop.

TOP RIGHT: Glass and stone are warmed by the mid-tone wood cabinetry. The structural sconces and elongated pulls add to the mid-century modern appeal.

BOTTOM RIGHT: From the hard edges of the showerhead and faucet to the boxy vanity and porcelain tiles, squares are simple but striking when repeated.

This primary bath is a worthy 21st century interpretation of modern design.

FAR RIGHT: Strong horizontal lines of the awning windows reflect the modern style. Above the tub and shower area, they provide both natural light and fresh air while protecting privacy.

TOP RIGHT: Sea-green glass and limestone tiles in the walk-in shower and tub wall add subdued color.

it's in the DETAILS

BOTTOM RIGHT: Above the vanity, with its polished limestone counter, a striking ebony-colored recessed wall is the backdrop for simple faucets and unframed mirrors that hang from metal rods. The compact fluorescent light fixtures have been mounted directly on the glass.

Natural Beauty

Organic modern style has skyrocketed onto the scene in recent years, but its roots in modern and Scandinavian styles have been in the home for decades. Related to biophilic design—an architectural, decorative, and design philosophy that creates human connections with the outdoors and nature—this style features both physical and aesthetic ties to nature. Think bathrooms that open to the outdoors, outdoor showers, and large windows with views of trees, water, and plant life.

The look favors clean lines with pared-down furnishings—you'll see plenty of unadorned walls and large windows in these spaces. Natural materials like stone and wood are likely to be found on any—or every—surface, showcasing their textures and subtle patterns. Not strictly limited to the real deal, engineered stone and wood-look materials are equally welcome. Other organic elements like jute, rattan, and bamboo are also found accenting furniture, mirrors, or cabinetry.

Warm and cool neutrals combine for an earthy and sometimes spa-like palette. Rounded profiles and organic shapes are brought in to stand out against the otherwise straight lines of its modern foundation. From shining chrome to rich brass and warm bronze, metals accent and elevate the style.

FAR RIGHT: Less is more—at least in these spaces. This minimalist aesthetic lets the natural (and natural-looking) materials and architecture speak for themselves. Greenery, however, is always a welcome accent.

RIGHT: Multiple showerheads and an accordion door let you create your own experience in this spacious shower. Notice the textures of the stone floor that bring the outside to the interior.

Abundant white surfaces reflect natural light, so this simple space feels warm and bright.

FAR RIGHT: Windows above the bathing area offer a connection to the outdoors without sacrificing privacy. Touches of greenery, also integral to organic style, pop against the bath's neutral colors.

TOP RIGHT: Opposite the shower and tub, a storage wall features a floating double vanity and floor-to-ceiling cabinets built into the walls. High mirrors reflect the natural light from the windows.

it's in the DETAILS

MIDDLE RIGHT: Simple lines are repeated in the linear cabinet hardware and sconces, rectangular and wood panels.

BOTTOM RIGHT: Limited to the generous tub and shower area, wood panels offer showstopping texture and bring the outdoors in. With plenty of care and maintenance, they can thrive in the bath.

DESIGN BY MEL BEAN INTERIORS, PHOTOGRAPHY BY LAUREY GLENN.

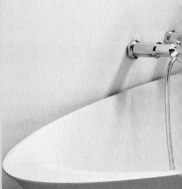

SMART APPROACH: WORK WITH COLOR

GET INSPIRED

Look at the world around you. For an explosion of color, visit the produce aisle of the grocery store. Comb through fashion magazines and art books. Look at your own closet: see a repeated color? That's a hint that you're naturally drawn to it.

Do you want the bath to energize you at the start of the day? Relax you at the end of the week? Exploring color theory can help you narrow your focus, too. The color wheel is another resource. You can find analogous and complementing colors for an idea of what may work together, or it can help you decide a second color to complement what you've already chosen.

DISTRIBUTE COLOR EFFECTIVELY

Color distribution helps a room look put together. 70/20/10 is a classic way to proportion color. For example, apply a neutral to 70 percent of the room, a rich chosen color to 20 percent, and a bold accent to only 10 percent. If you're using two colors, divide the space in a 70/30 distribution. The rule of three also helps apply color. Using a color at least three times in the space—like towels, accent tile, and a painted vanity—will help the color choice look intentional.

DON'T FORGET THE NEUTRALS

Color isn't just about pinks, blues, and greens. Neutrals help balance color in the room, as well as give the eye a resting place. This is why a bold pattern or color in a small space doesn't feel overwhelming—usually there's a neutral element to ease the overall feel. Sometimes lighting and plumbing fixture finishes, like chrome or gold, can act as a neutral.

Also, remember to consider sources of neutral colors that may already be present in the room. The hues in wood vanities, stone flooring, even baseboards and tubs can be easily overlooked, but still play a part in your color palette. Whether these shades are cool or warm can also have an impact.

ELEVATE A MONOCHROMATIC SCHEME

If too many colors are your personal nightmare, there are many ways to make a monochromatic space stylish. Whether it's a warm gray, deep blue, or a crisp white, you can—and should—give a one-hued-room depth and dimension. Start by incorporating textured materials and mixing matte and polished finishes. You can also find ways to incorporate patterns: instead of square floor tiles, a basketweave in matching tile and grout is a monochromatic choice that still offers pleasing visual interest. Also consider using the color in multiple shades or varying saturations for a fresh, not dull, overall look.

RESOURCE GUIDE

The following list of manufacturers and associations is meant to be a general guide to additional industry and product-related sources. It is not intended as a listing of products and manufacturers represented by the photographs in this book.

Manufacturers

Accessible Environments, Inc.
800-643-5906
www.acessinc.com
Sells handicap-accessible products.

American Standard
800-442-1902
www.americanstandard-us.com
Manufactures plumbing and tile products.

Ann Sacks Tile and Stone
part of the Kohler Company
800-278-8453
www.annsacks.com
Manufactures a broad line of tile and stone, including terra-cotta and mosaics.

Armstrong World Industries
877-276-7876
www.armstrong.com
Manufactures floors, cabinets, and ceilings for both residential and commercial use.

Artemide
877-278-9111
www.artemide.com
Manufactures lighting fixtures.

Artistic Tile
877-237-4097
www.artistictile.com
Offers different types of tile, including those made of stone, ceramic, glass, metal, cement, and cork.

BainUltra
(also known as Ultra Bath)
800-463-2187
www.ultrabath.com
Manufactures a luxury line of bathtubs that offer a hydro-therapeutic massage.

Bemis Manufacturing Co.
920-467-4621
www.bemismfg.com
Manufactures toilet seats.

Benjamin Moore & Co.
www.benjaminmoore.com
Manufactures paint.

Broan-NuTone® LLC
www.broan-nutone.com
North America's fresh air leader, manufacturing and distributing residential ventilation and built-in convenience products, including range hoods, ventilation fans, air purifiers and central vacuum systems.

CaesarStone USA
818-779-0999
www.caesarstoneus.com
Manufactures quartz-composite countertops.

Carrara Tiles
888-422-4655
www.carraratiles.com
Distributes slate and granite slabs and tile.

CertainTeed
800-233-8990
www.certainteed.com
Manufactures building products.

ClosetMaid
800-874-0008
www.closetmaid.com
Produces home storage and organization systems.

The Container Store
888-266-8246
www.thecontainerstore.com
Sells storage and organization products.

Contrast Lighting
888-839-4624
www.contrastlighting.com
Manufactures recessed lighting, suspension lamps, and wall and ceiling fixtures.

Cooper Lighting
www.cooperindustries.com
Manufactures lighting products.

Corian
division of DuPont
www.corian.com
Manufactures solid-surfacing material
for residential and commercial
kitchens.

Cosentino
cosentino.com/usa
Manufactures innovative architectural
surfacing solutions including
Silestone® and Dekton®.

Dal-Tile
www.daltile.com
Manufactures ceramic and stone tile.

Dex Industries
404-753-0600
www.dexstudios.com
Creates custom concrete sinks and
countertops.

eFaucets
855-853-0161
www.efaucets.com
Online retailer of bathroom and
kitchen faucets, sinks, and accessories.

Emser Tile
323-650-2000
www.emser.com
Leading designer, marketer and
producer of the world's finest tile and
natural stone.

Formica Corp.
800-367-6422
www.formica.com
Manufactures plastic laminate and
solid-surfacing material.

Ginger
949-417-5207
www.gingerco.com
Manufactures lighting and bathroom
accessories.

Herbeau Creations of America
239-417-5368
www.herbeau.com
Makes vitreous-china fixtures.

Hoesch Design
www.hoesch.de
Manufactures tubs and shower
partitions.

Hunter Douglas
1-800-789-0331
www.hunterdouglas.com
Manufactures custom-made window
treatments.

Jaclo
800-852-3906
www.jaclo.com
Manufactures showerheads and body
sprays.

Jacuzzi Whirlpool Bath
www.jacuzzi.com
Manufactures jetted tubs and
showers.

Kallista
888-452-5547
www.kallista.com
Manufactures plumbing products
such as faucets, showerheads, and
sinks.

Kichler Lighting
866-558-5706
www.kichler.com
Manufactures decorative light
fixtures, lamps, and home accessories.

Kohler
800-456-4537
www.kohler.com
Manufactures kitchen and bath sinks,
faucets, and related accessories.

KraftMaid Cabinetry
888-562-7744
www.kraftmaid.com
Manufactures stock and built-to-
order cabinets with a variety of
finishes and storage options.

Lasco
717-367-1100
www.lascobathware.net
Makes barrier-free showers.

Legrand
877-295-3472
www.legrand.us
Legrand is a world-renowned
specialist in electrical wiring devices

Lightology
866-954-4489
www.lightology.com
Manufactures lighting fixtures.

Maestro Mosaics
312-670-4400
Supplies and installs stone and glass
tile.

Majestic Shower Co.
800-675-6225
www.calshowerdoor.com
Manufactures showers and glass-door
enclosures.

Mannington, Inc.
800-356-6787
www.mannington.com
Manufactures residential and
commercial flooring products.

Mansfield Plumbing Products
877-850-3060
www.mansfieldplumbing.com
Manufactures toilets, lavs, bathtubs, and whirlpools.

Merillat
866-850-8557
www.merillat.com
Manufactures cabinets.

MGS Progetti
www.mgstaps.com
Manufactures stainless-steel faucets.

Minka Group
951-735-9220
www.minkagroup.net
Designs contemporary lighting products.

Moen
800-289-6636
www.moen.com
Manufactures faucets, sinks, and accessories for both kitchens and baths.

Mosaic & Tile Source Inc.
888-669-4233
www.mosaicsource.ca
Online source for mosaic and recycled-glass tiles.

Motif Designs
800-431-2424
www.motif-designs.com
Manufactures furniture, fabrics, and wall coverings.

**Mr. Sauna, Inc.,
and Mr. Steam, Inc.**
part of the Sussman Lifestyle Group
800-767-8326
www.mrsteam.com
Manufactures saunas and sauna products.

MrSteam
1-800-76-STEAM (78326)
https://www.mrsteam.com/
MrSteam offers innovative new high-tech swipe-touch controls, such as iSteamX, advanced steam shower generators and systems, soothing aromatherapy and ChromaTherapy, and smart home integration.

Nantucket Beadboard
603-330-1070
www.beadboard.com
Manufactures bead-board products.

Neo-Metro
division of Acorn Engineering Co.
800-591-9050
www.neo-metro.com
Manufactures countertops, tubs, lavs, and tile.

NuTone, Inc.
888-336-3948
www.nutone.com
Manufactures ventilation fans, medicine cabinets, and lighting fixtures.

Pfister Faucets
800-732-8238
www.pfisterfaucets.com
Manufactures faucets.

Porcelanosa
www.porcelanosa-usa.com
Manufactures marble and tile surfaces and mosaics.

Porcher
800-442-1902
www.porcher-us.com
Manufactures luxury plumbing fixtures.

Radiantec
800-451-7593
www.radiantec.com
Manufactures radiant-heating systems.

Robern
division of Kohler
800-877-2376
www.robern.com
Manufactures medicine cabinets and accessories.

Saunatec
888-780-4427
www.saunatec.com
Manufactures saunas, steam baths, sauna heaters, and other luxury bath items.

Seagull Lighting Products, Inc.
800-347-5483
www.seagulllighting.com
Manufactures lighting fixtures.

SFA Saniflo
www.saniflo.com
800-571-8191
Saniflo SFA, a division of Group SFA, is the world leader in residential and commercial above-the-floor macerating and grinding toilets systems, lift stations and gray-water pumps.

Sherwin-Williams
www.sherwin-williams.com
Manufactures paint.

Solar Screen
866-230-4700
www.northsolarscreen.com
Manufactures energy-efficient
window shades.

Sonia
www.sonia-sa.com
Manufactures bath fixtures.

Sonoma Cast Stone
877-939-9929
www.sonomastone.com
Designs and builds concrete sinks and
countertops.

Sterling Plumbing
800-783-7546
www.sterlingplumbing.com
Offers ADA-compliant bathroom
products.

Stone Forest
888-682-2987
www.stoneforest.com
Manufactures metal and stone
bathtubs and lavs.

Swarovski Lighting, Inc.
800-836-1892
www.swarovski-lighting.com
Manufactures crystal lighting
fixtures.

Thibaut Inc.
800-223-0704
www.thibautdesign.com
Manufactures wallpaper and fabrics.

Toto USA
888-295-8134
www.totousa.com
Manufactures toilets, bidets, sinks,
and bathtubs.

Tyrrell & Laing International Inc.
813-625-1178
www.tandlinternational.com
Manufactures luxury tubs.

US Block Windows
888-256-2599
www.hy-lite.com
Manufactures acrylic and glass-block
windows.

Velux
800-888-3589
www.veluxusa.com
Manufactures skylights and solar
tunnels.

Villeroy & Boch
800-845-5376
www.villeroy-boch.com
Manufactures china fixtures.

VitrA
www.vitraglobal.com
Manufactures products and
accessories for the bath.

Waterworks
800-899-6757
www.waterworks.com
Manufactures plumbing products.

Wetstyle
888-536-9001
www.wetstyle.ca
Manufactures bath fixtures.

Whirlpool Corp.
866-698-2538
www.whirlpool.com
Manufactures major home appliances.

Wilsonart International, Inc.
800-433-3222
www.wilsonart.com
Manufactures solid-surfacing
material; plastic laminate; and
adhesive for countertops, cabinets,
floors, and fixtures.

**Wood-Mode Fine Custom
Cabinetry**
www.wood-mode.com
Manufactures semicustom cabinetry.

York Wallcoverings
717-846-4456
www.yorkwallcoverings.com
Manufactures a wide variety of
wallcoverings, including murals
and traditional and peel-and-stick
wallpapers; offers online tips, advice,
and how-to.

Zodiaq
division of DuPont
www.zodiaq.com
Manufactures quartz-composite
countertops.

Associations

American Institute of Architetcts (AIA)
800-242-3837
www.aia.org
A professional membership organization for licensed architects, emerging professionals, and allied partners.

American Society of Interior Designers (ASID)
202-546-3480
www.asid.org
A community committed to interior design and its positive effect on people's lives.

Ceramic Tile Institute of America (CTIOA)
310-574-7800
www.ctioa.org
A trade organization that promotes the ceramic tile industry. Its Web site provides consumer information about ceramic tile.

Forest Stewardship Council of the United States (FSCUS)
612-353-4511
www.fscus.org
A professional organization coordinating the development of forest-management standards.

International Interior Design Association (IIDA)
888-799-4432
www.iida.org
A professional organization facilitating a community of interior design professionals.

National Association of Remodeling Industry (NARI)
847-298-9200
www.nari.org
A professional organization for remodelers, contractors, and design/remodelers; also offers consumer information.

National Kitchen and Bath Association (NKBA)
800-843-6522
www.nkba.org
A national trade organization for kitchen and bath design professionals; offers consumers product information and a referral service.

Tile Council of America
864-646-8453
www.tileusa.com
A trade organization dedicated to promoting the tile industry; also provides consumer information on selecting and installing tile.

Designers

Golden Rule Builders
(540) 788-3539
www.GoldenRuleBuilders.com

Helene Goodman, IIDA Interior Design
732-747-8502
www.helenegoodmaninteriordesign.com
h.goodman@comcast.net

Lucianna Samu
www.luciannasamu.com
lu@luciannasamu.com

Mary Patton Design
https://www.marypattondesign.com/
hello@marypattondesign.com

Mel Bean Interiors
www.melbeaninteriors.com
Design@melbeaninteriors.com

Plural Design Studio
www.pluraldesignstudio.com
612-296-7804

Susan Obercian European Country Kitchens
www.susanoberciandesign.com
sobercian@me.com

GLOSSARY

Absorption (light): The energy (wavelengths) not reflected by an object or substance. The color of a substance depends on the wavelength reflected.

Accent lighting: A type of light that highlights an area or object to emphasize that aspect of a room's character.

Accessible design: Design that accommodates persons with physical disabilities.

Accessories: Towel racks, soap dishes, and other items specifically designed for use in the bath.

Adaptable design: Design that can be easily changed to accommodate a person with disabilities.

Ambient light: General illumination that fills a room. There is no visible source of the light.

Antiscalding valve (pressure-balancing valve): A single-control fitting that contains a piston that automatically responds to changes in line water pressure to maintain temperature; the valve blocks an abrupt drop or rise in temperature.

Apron: The front extension of a bathtub that runs from the rim to the floor.

Awning window: A window with a single framed-glass panel. It is hinged at the top to swing out when it is open.

Backlighting: Illumination coming from a source behind or at the side of an object.

Backsplash: The finish material that covers the wall behind a countertop. The backsplash can be attached to the countertop or separate from it.

Barn door: Sliding barn doors are great for adding style and also save space.

Barrier-free fixtures: Fixtures specifically designed for disabled individuals who use wheelchairs or who have limited mobility.

Baseboard: A trim board attached as part of a base treatment to the bottom of a wall where it meets the floor.

Base cabinet: A cabinet that rests on the floor under a countertop or vanity.

Base plan: A map of an existing bathroom that shows detailed measurements and the location of fixtures and their permanent elements.

Basin: A shallow sink.

Bidet: A bowl-shaped fixture that supplies water for personal hygiene. It looks similar to a toilet.

Body spray: Water- and air-jet sprays housed behind the shower walls, much like those used in whirlpool tubs.

Built-in: A cabinet, shelf, medicine chest, or other storage unit that is recessed into the wall.

Bump out: Living space created by cantilevering the floor and ceiling joists (or adding to a floor slab) and extending the exterior wall of a room.

Cantilever: A structural beam supported on one end. A cantilever can be used to support a bump out.

Casement window: A window that consists of one framed-glass panel that is hinged on the side. It swings outward from the opening at the turn of a crank.

Casing: The general term for any trim that surrounds a window.

Centerline: The dissecting line that runs through the center of an object, such as a sink.

Center-set faucets: Have two separate valves (one for hot, another for cold) and a spout that are connected in one unit. There are four inches between the two handles.

CFM: An abbreviation that refers to the amount of cubic feet of air that is moved per minute by an exhaust fan.

Chair rail: A decorative wall molding installed midway between the floor and ceiling. Traditionally, chair rails protected walls from damage from chair backs.

Clearance: The amount of space between two fixtures, the centerlines of two fixtures, or a fixture and an obstacle, such as a wall. Clearances may be mandated by building codes.

Code: A locally or nationally enforced mandate regarding structural design, materials, plumbing, or electrical systems that states what you can or cannot do when you build or remodel. Codes are intended to protect standards of health, safety, and land use.

Contemporary style: A style of decoration or architecture that is modern and pertains to what is current.

Corner fixtures: Showers, lavs, vanities, and toilets designed to tuck neatly into a corner are great solutions for small bathrooms or powder rooms.

Cornice: Any molding or group of moldings used in the corner between a wall and a ceiling.

Countertop: The work surface of a counter, usually 36 inches high. Common countertop materials include stone, plastic laminate, ceramic tile, concrete, and solid surfacing.

Cove lights: Lights that reflect upward, sometimes located on top of wall cabinets.

Crown molding: A decorative molding usually installed where the wall and ceiling meet.

Curbless shower: Also called a zero-threshold or barrier-free shower. This accessible design doesn't have a raised threshold you must step over to enter the shower.

Dimmer switch: A switch that can vary the intensity of the light source that it controls.

Door casing: The trim applied to a wall around the edge of a door frame.

Double-glazed window: A window consisting of two panes of glass separated by a space that contains air or argon gas. The space provides most of the insulation.

Double-hung window: A window that consists of two framed-glass panels that slide open vertically, guided by a metal or wood track.

Downlighting: A lighting technique that illuminates objects or areas from above.

Duct: A tube or passage for venting indoor air to the outside.

Enclosure: Any material used to form a shower or tub stall, such as glass, glass block, or a tile wall.

Fittings: The plumbing devices that transport water to the fixtures. These can include showerheads, faucets, and spouts. Also pertains to hardware and some accessories, such as towel racks, soap dishes, and toilet-paper dispensers.

Fixed spray: Attached to a shower arm and mounted to the wall or ceiling, fixed sprays can have a large head and spray area.

Fixed window: A window that cannot be opened. It is usually a decorative unit, such as a half-round or Palladian-style window.

Fixture: Any fixed part of the structural design, such as tubs, bidets, toilets, and lavatories.

Fixture spacing: The amount of space included between ambient light fixtures to achieve an even field of illumination in a given area.

Fluorescent lamp: An energy-efficient light source made of a tube with an interior phosphorus coating that glows when energized by electricity.

Form: The shape and structure of space or an object.

Full bath: A bath that includes a toilet, lavatory, and bathing fixture, such as a tub or shower.

Glass blocks: Decorative building blocks made of translucent glass used for non-load-bearing walls to allow passage of light.

Grab bare: A safety feature to help someone maintain balance and safely navigate in areas, such as the shower or toilet area.

Ground-fault circuit interrupter (GFCI): A safety circuit breaker that compares the amount of current entering a receptacle with the amount leaving. If there is a discrepancy of 0.005 volt, the GFCI breaks the circuit in a fraction of a second. GFCIs are required by the National Electrical Code in areas of the house that are subject to dampness.

Grout: A binder and filler applied in the joints between ceramic tile.

Half bath (powder room): A bathroom that contains only a toilet and a sink.

Handheld spray: A device that's convenient for directing water where you want it. It's connected to a wall-mounted slide bar or mounted and used like a traditional fixed spray showerhead, but on a removable cradle. Tubs can also have a handheld spray fixture.

Highlight: The lightest tone in a room.

Integral lav: As the word "integral" implies, the sink and countertop are fabricated from the same material, such as stone or solid surfacing.

Intensity: Strength of a color.

Jamb: The frame around a window or door.

Jets: Nozzles installed behind the walls of tubs or showers that pump out pressurized streams of water.

Joist: Set in a parallel fashion, these framing members support the boards of a ceiling or a floor.

Laminate: A surface material made of layers of melamine, paper, and plastic resin that are bonded under heat and pressure and then glued to particleboard or plywood.

Lavatory or lav: A fixed bowl or basin with running water and a drainpipe that is used for washing.

Load-bearing wall: A wall that supports a structure's vertical load. Openings in any load-bearing wall must be reinforced to carry the live and dead weight of the structure's load.

Macerating toilet: A type of toilet that utilizes a macerator to grind waste and a pump to move the waste up to your main plumbing stack (they're also called upflush toilets).

Medallion: A decorative, usually round relief, carving applied to a wall.

Molding: Decorative strips of wood or plastic used in various kinds of trimwork.

Muntins: Framing members of a window that divide the panes of glass.

Nonbearing wall: A wall that does not support the weight of areas above it.

On center: A point of reference for measuring. For example, "16 inches on center" means 16 inches from the center of one framing member to the center of the next.

Overflow: An outlet positioned in a tub or sink that allows water to escape if a faucet is left open.

Palette: A range of colors that complement each other.

Pedestal: A stand-alone lavatory with a basin and supporting column in one piece.

Pocket door: A door that opens by sliding inside the wall, as opposed to a conventional door that opens into a room.

Pressure-balancing valve: Also known as a surge protector or antiscalding device. It is a control that prevents surges of hot or cold water in faucets by equalizing the amounts of hot and cold water pumped out at any time.

Primary bath: A bathroom that is either connected to the largest (or primary) bedroom in the house. Sometimes called an "en suite bathroom," a primary bath is a full bathroom or a three-quarter bathroom. It's also known as a master bathroom.

Proportion: The relationship of one object to another.

Quartzite: A natural stone that is popular for surfacing, particularly countertops.

Radiant floor heat: A type of heating that is brought into a room via electrical wire or pipes (to carry hot water) that have been installed under the floor. As the pipes or electrical wire heats up, the flooring material warms and heat rises into the room.

Rail: Horizontal trimwork installed on a wall between the cornice and base trim. It may stand alone, as a chair rail, or be part of a larger framework.

Reflectance levels: The amount of light that is reflected from a colored surface, such as a tile wall or painted surface.

Resilient flooring: Thin floor coverings composed of materials such as vinyl, rubber, cork, or linoleum. Comes in a wide range of colors and patterns in both tile and sheet forms.

Rimmed lav: Unlike a self-rimming sink, this type requires a metal strip to form the seal between the top of the sink and the countertop.

Roof window: A horizontal window that is installed on the roof. Roof windows are ventilating.

Roughing-in: The installation of the water-supply and DWV (drain-waste-vent) pipes before the fixtures are in place.

Rubber float: A flat, rubber-faced tool used to apply grout.

Scale: The size of a room or object.

Sconce: A decorative wall bracket, sometimes made of iron or glass, which shields a bulb.

Self-rimming lav: Also called a drop-in sink, the bowl is surface-mounted—you drop it into the counter, and the ridge forms a seal with the countertop surface.

Sight line: The natural line of sight the eye travels along when looking into or around a room.

Single-lever faucets: A faucet with a spout and single lever in one piece.

Sintered stone: A new, engineered stone surfacing material created from minerals and other materials.

Skylight: A framed opening in the roof that admits sunlight into the house. It can be covered with either a flat glass panel or a plastic dome.

Sliding window: Similar to a double-hung window turned on its side. The glass panels slide horizontally.

Soffit: A boxed-in area just below the ceiling and above the vanity.

Solar tunnel: Also called a tubular skylight, this shaft makes it possible to bring natural light into a room.

Solid surfacing: A synthetic surfacing material made of polyester or acrylic.

Spa: An inground or aboveground tublike structure or vessel that is equipped with whirlpool jets.

Space reconfiguration: A design term that is used to describe the reallocation of interior space without adding on.

Spout: The tube or pipe from which water gushes out of a faucet.

Steam shower: A tightly enclosed shower that delivers steam from a generator, in addition to the traditional shower experience.

Stock cabinets: Cabinets that are in stock or available quickly when ordered from a retail outlet.

Stops: On doors, the trim on the jamb that keeps the door from swinging through; on windows, the trim that covers the inside face of the jamb.

Stud: The vertical member of a frame wall placed at both ends and usually every 16 inches on center. A stud provides structural framing and facilitates covering with drywall or plywood.

Surround: The enclosure and area around a tub or shower. A surround may include steps and a platform, as well as the tub itself.

Task lighting: Lighting designed to illuminate a particular task, such as shaving.

Three-quarter bath: A bathroom that contains a toilet, sink, and shower.

Tone: The degree of lightness or darkness of a color.

Traditional style: A style of decoration or architecture (typically of the eighteenth and nineteenth centuries) that employs forms that have been repeated for generations without major changes.

Under-mounted lav: The sink is attached underneath the countertop for a sleek, rimless appearance.

Universal design: Products and designs that are easy to use by people of all ages, heights, and varying physical abilities.

Vanity: The countertop and cabinet unit that supports a sink. The vanity is usually included in the bathroom for storage purposes. It may also be used as a dressing table.

Ventilation: The process of removing or supplying air to a certain space.

Vessel lav: An above-counter sink that sits much like a bowl on a table.

Vinyl: A budget-friendly surface option, made from synthetic materials, that's water resistant and stain proof.

Whirlpool: A special tub that includes motorized jets behind the walls of the tub for water massages.

Widespread faucets: Feature a spout with separate hot- and cold-water valves. All appear to be completely separate pieces.

Index

A

accessibility
  finding builders/designers for, 26
  lighting and, 168
  planning for, 21, 54–56
  showers, faucets and, 54, 55, 80, 81, 89
  storage, 54, 136, 139, 144, 148
  vanities, 134
acrylic countertops, 119, 134
acrylic tubs/surrounds, 72, 74, 120
adjacent half-baths, 48
air quality. *See* ventilation
American Institute of Architects (AIA), 26
American Society of Interior Designers (ASID), 26
Americans with Disabilities Act, 34
angled bathtubs, 46
antibacterial surfaces, 118
antique dressers, 61, 140
architects, 20, 26, 38
archway, 41
artificial lighting, 156–59
assessing needs, 14–16
attic, basement, closet baths, 62–65

B

base plan/map, 40
basement, attic, closet baths, 62–65
bathrooms. *See also* primary baths
  children and, 52
  family, 53
  furniture for, 140–43
  half, 48, 58–59, 60–61
  partial, 58–61
  planning storage for, 125–27

  shared, 52–56
  sprucing up old, 92
  three-quarter, 58, 59
bathtubs. *See* tubs
beadboard, 104, 192–93
bidet seats, 70, 71, 91
body sprays, 82
budgeting, 20
building codes, 25, 32, 38, 40, 170
building permits, 21, 25, 32
built-in storage, 42, 56, 129, 136, 140, 141, 145
built-in vanities, 130

C

cabin spa, 50
cabinets. *See also* medicine cabinets; vanities
  built-in, 56, 140, 145
  hardware, 54, 117, 132, 181, 182, 190, 194, 200
  linen storage, 144–49
  organizing steps, 148
  painted, 190
  stock, 134
  storage planning, 128–29
Carrara tiles, 18
cement tile, 110
ceramic tile. *See* tiles
Certified Aging in Place Specialists (CAPS), 26
Certified Bath Designers (CBDs), 26
Certified Living in Place Professional (CLIPP), 26
change orders, 30, 33
chic retreat, 178–79
children, baths for, 52, 134

Clawfoot tubs, 192
closet, basement, attic baths, 62–65
closet, walk-in, 44
color, design guidelines, 202–3
color schemes, monochromatic, 56, 160, 203
concrete surfaces, 102, 103. *See also* cement tile
contemporary style, 194
contractors
  interviewing several, 21
  knowing what they do, 26
  selecting, 26
  signing for deliveries by, 29
contracts, about, 28–30
convection heat, 174
corner fixtures, 43, 58, 59
cottage style, 190–93
countertops, 114–19

D

debt-to-income (DTI) ratio, 23
deliveries, accepting, 29
design-build remodeling firms, 26
do-it-yourself questionnaire, 26
doors
  pocket, 40, 51, 57
  sliding screens and, 14, 42
double showers, 50
double vanities/sinks, 30–31, 47, 49, 52, 126, 131, 136, 144
drains
  linear, 70, 71, 84, 107
  location tip, 63
dry sink, 131

PHOTO CREDITS

Front cover: *top* Mel Bean Interiors, photography: Laurey Glenn *bottom left* Broan-NuTone *bottom middle* Mary Patton Design, photography: Molly Culver *bottom right* Broan-NuTone **page 2:** Mel Bean Interiors, photography: Kacey Gilpin **pages 4–5:** Emser Tile **pages 6–7:** davidduncanlivingston.com **pages 8–9:** Mark Samu, design/architect: Andrea Letkovsky AIA **pages 10–11:** *left* Mark Lohman, design: Malibu Interiors & Design; *right* Dekton by Cosentino **pages 12–13:** Eric Roth **pages 14–15:** *all* davidduncanlivingston.com **page 16:** Mary Patton Design, photography: Molly Culver **page 17:** *top right* Eric Roth, design: ruhlwalker.com *bottom right* Kohler **pages 18–19** *all* Mark Samu, design/architect: Andrea Letkovsky AIA **page 20:** *top* Kohler *bottom* Mark Lohman **page 21:** Dekton by Cosetino **pages 22–23:** *all* Bob Greenspan, stylist: Susan Andrews **page 24:** *top right* davidduncanlivingston.com *bottom left* York Wallcoverings **page 26:** Kohler **page 27:** *top left* davidduncanlivingston.com *bottom left* Kohler *right* davidduncanlivingston.com **pages 28–29:** *top middle* Johnny Bouchier/Red Cover; bottom left Eric Roth, design: fbnconstruction.net; *bottom right* Wetstyle **pages 30–31:** Julian Wass, design: Hein + Cozzi Inc. **pages 32–33:** *left* Mark Lohman, design: Taddey & Karlin Design *middle* Mark Lohman, design: Janet Lohman Interior Design *right* Mark Lohman **pages 34–35:** *all* Eric Roth, design: bkarch.com **pages 36–37:** Kohler **page 38:** Mel Bean Interiors, photography: Laurey Glenn **page 39:** MrSteam **page 41:** Plural Design Studio, photography and styling: Mallory Lunke, contractor: Lind Nelson Construction **page 42:** *left* Mark Lohman, design: GSGibson Inc. *right* Eric Roth, design: christofiinteriors. com **page 43:** *left* Jerry Pavia *right* Eric Roth, design: John DeBastiani **page 44:** Eric Roth, design: Elisa Allen Interiors **page 45:** Eric Roth, design: christinetuttle.com **page 47:** *top* Anne Gummerson, design: kitchensbyrequest. com *bottom* Karyn Millet/Red Cover, design: The Warwick Group **page 49:** *top left* Bob Greenspan, stylist: Susan Andrews *top right* Eric Roth, design/build:

jwconstructioninc.com *bottom* Mark Samu, design: Evergreen Interiors **pages 50–51:** *all* davidduncanlivingston.com **page 52:** *top* Mark Samu *bottom* davidduncanlivingston.com **page 54:** *top* Bob Greenspan, stylist: Susan Andrews, design: Elizabeth Goltz, designbyorion.com *bottom* Legrand **page 55:** *top* melabee m miller, design: Nancee Brown, ASID *bottom* Mark Lohman, design: Janet Lohman Interior Design **pages 56–57:** *all* Golden Rule Builders, photography: Kaan Ozturk **page 58:** *left* Plural Design Studio, photography and styling: Mallory Lunke *right* davidduncanlivingston. com **page 60:** *bottom left* Kichler Lighting *top right* York Wallcoverings *middle* Olson Photographic, LLC, design: Capitol Designs **page 61:** Eric Roth, design: John DeBastiani **page 62:** *all* SFA Saniflo, artist: Servex **page 63:** Artazum / Shutterstock **page 64:** *left* Kristen Prahl / Shutterstock *right* United Photo Studio / Shutterstock **page 65:** Eric Roth, design: heidipribell.com **pages 66–67:** Olson Photographic, LLC, design/builder: Timberdale Homes **pages 68–69:** *all* Mary Patton Design, photography: Molly Culver **page 70:** *top* Kohler *bottom* Golden Rule Builders, photography: Kaan Ozturk **page 71:** *top left* Golden Rule Builders, photography: Kaan Ozturk *top right* MrSteam *bottom right* Golden Rule Builders, photography: Kaan Ozturk **page 72:** *top* Mark Samu, architect: Ellen Roche AIA *bottom* York Wallcoverings **page 73:** *top* Kohler *bottom* Hastings Tile & Bath **pages 74–75:** *middle* York Wallcoverings *top right* Corian *bottom right* Broan-NuTone **page 76:** *left* Mary Patton Design, photography: Molly Culver *top right* Tony Giammarino/Giammarino & Dworkin, design: SandraVitzthum.com *middle right* Kohler *bottom right* Kohler **page 77:** *left* davidduncanlivingston.com *right* MGSProgetti.com **pages 78–79:** all Olson Photographic, LLC, design: Stacey Gendelman Designs **pages 80–81:** *top middle* Golden Rule Builders, photography: Kaan Ozturk *bottom left* Karyn Millet/Red Cover, design: Molly Isaksen *bottom middle* Eric Roth, design: ruhlwalker.com *bottom right* MrSteam **page 82:** *all*

Kohler **page 83:** davidduncanlivingston.com **pages 84–85:** *all* Golden Rule Builders, photography: Linda Andersson **pages 86–87:** *bottom left* Silestone by Cosetino *top middle* Joseph De Leo *top right* davidduncanlivingston.com *bottom middle* Kichler Lighting *bottom right* Eric Roth, design: jwconstructioninc.com **page 88:** *left* Kohler *right* Eric Roth, design/architect: spacecraftarch.com **page 89:** *top left* Mel Bean Interiors, photography: Kacey Gilpin *top right* Mary Patton Design, photography: Molly Culver *bottom* Kohler **page 90:** *left* Eric Roth, design: mtruant.com *right* Kohler **page 91:** *left* Plural Design Studio, photography and styling: Mallory Lunke, contractor: Lind Nelson Construction *right* Kohler **page 92:** *left* Eric Roth, design: Planeta Basque Boston LLC *right* Stacy Bass **page 93:** *left* Eric Roth, design: paynebouchier.com *right* Kohler **pages 94–95:** Kohler **pages 96–97:** *left* Dekton by Cosentino *middle top* Stacy Bass *top right* Emser Tile *bottom right* Silestone by Cosentino **pages 98–99:** *bottom left* Mark Lohman, design: Lynn Pries Design *top middle* Dekton by Cosentino *top right* Emser Tile *bottom right* davidduncanlivingston.com **page 100:** *left* Mark Lohman, architect: Michael Lee Architects *right* Mark Lohman, design: William Hefner Inc. **page 101:** Mark Lohman, design: Janet Lohman Interior Design **page 102:** Dekton by Cosentino **page 103:** *top* Dekton by Cosentino *bottom left* Eric Roth, design: christofiinteriors.com *bottom right* Paul Ryan-Goff/Red Cover **page 104:** *left* Eric Roth, design: Elisa Allen Interiors *right* York Wallcoverings **page 105:** Broan-NuTone **page 106–107:** *middle* melabee m miller, design: Tammy Kaplan *top* Olson Photographic, LLC, design/build: Hobbs, Inc. *bottom* davidduncanlivingston.com **page 108:** Emser Tile **page 109:** *top* Mel Bean Interiors, photography: Laurey Glenn *bottom left* Plural Design Studio, photography and styling: Mallory Lunke, contractor: Lind Nelson Construction *bottom right* Mark Lohman, design: Janet Lohman Interior Design **page 110:** Eric Roth, left design: mtruant.com **page 111:** *top* Mary Patton Design, photography: Molly Culver *bottom left* Tony Giammarino/Giammarino & Dworkin, design/architect: evolvearchitecture.com *bottom right* Mel Bean Interiors, photography: Laurey Glenn **pages 112–113:** *all* Plural Design Studio, photography and styling: Mallory Lunke, contractor: Lind Nelson Construction **page 114:** Silestone by Cosentino **page 115:** *top* Mark Samu, design: Bonacio Construction *left* Eric Roth, design: Planeta Basque Boston LLC *right* Eric Roth **page 116:** Caesarstone **page 117:** *top* Silestone by Cosentino *bottom* Mary Patton Design, photography: Molly Culver **page 118:** StudioDin / Shutterstock **page 119:** *top left* Icestone / Shutterstock *top right* timltv / Shutterstock *bottom* davidduncanlivingston. com **page 120:** Golden Rule Builders, photography: Kaan Ozturk **page 121:** *top* melabee m miller, design: Nancee Brown, ASID *bottom* Anne Gummerson, design: Rhea Arnot Design **page 122:** *left* Kohler *right* Emser Tile **page 123:** *left* Tony Giammarino/Giammarino & Dworkin, design/architect: evolvearchitecture.com *right* Eric Roth, design: trikeenan.com **pages 124–125:** Mark Lohman, design: GSGibson Inc. **page 126:** Eric Roth, design: daherinteriordesign.com **page 127:** Mark Lohman, design: William Hefner Inc. **pages 128–129:** *middle* Mel Bean Interiors, photography: Laurey Glenn *right* Mark Lohman, design: Taddey & Karlin Design **page 130:** Stacey Bass **page 131:** *top* Olson Photographic, LLC, design/build: Ricci Construction *left* Eric Roth, design: baypointbuilderscorp.com *right* Mel Bean Interiors, photography: Laurey Glenn **page 132:** Eric Roth **page 133:** *top left* Olson Photography, LLC, architect: Peter Cadoux Architects *top right* Kraftmaid *bottom* melabee m miller, design: Tammy Kaplan **page 134:** *left* davidduncanlivingston.com *right* Eric Roth **page 135:** *top* Silestone by Cosetino *bottom* Mary Patton Design, photography: Molly Culver **pages 136–137:** *all* Mel Bean Interiors, photography: Laurey Glenn **page 138:** *left* Olson Photographic, LLC, design/build: Coastal Point Development *top* New Africa Studio / Shutterstock *bottom* Mark Lohman **page 139:** Mark Lohman **page 140:** davidduncanlivingston.com **page 141:** *top left* Merillat *top right* Bob Greenspan, stylist: Susan Andrews *bottom* York Wallcoverings **pages 142–143:** *all* Kohler (featuring Simplice faucet and accessory collection) **page 144:** Eric Roth, design/build: howelldesignbuild.com **page 145:** *top* Stacy Bass *bottom* davidduncanlivingston.com **pages 146–**

147: *all* Tony Giammarino/Giammarino & Dworkin, design: LeslieStephensDesign.net **page 148:** *all* Merillat **page 149:** Emser Tile **pages 150–151:** Kichler Lighting **page 152:** *left* Eric Roth, design: svdesign.com *right* Eric Roth, design: zeroenergy.com **page 153:** Mary Patton Design, photography: Molly Culver **pages 154–155:** *all* davidduncanlivingston.com **page 156:** *left* melabee m miller, design: Nancee Brown, ASID *right* York Wallcoverings **page 157:** Kichler Lighting **page 158:** *left* Kichler Lighting *top* Julian Wass, design: Angie Hranowski Design Studio *bottom* Broan-NuTone **page 159:** davidduncanlivingston.com **page 160:** *left* Mark Lohman, design: GSGibson Inc. *right* Plural Design Studio, photography and styling: Mallory Lunke **page 161:** Mary Patton Design, photography: Molly Culver **page 162:** davidduncanlivingston.com **page 163:** davidduncanlivingston.com **pages 164–165:** *all* Golden Rule Builders, photography: Kaan Ozturk **page 166:** Olson Photographic, LLC, design/build: Hobbs, Inc. **page 167:** *top right* davidduncanlivingston.com *bottom left* davidduncanlivingston.com **page 168:** *left* Mark Samu *right* Legrand **page 169:** Mel Bean Interiors, photography: Laurey Glenn **page 170:** *left* Mark Lohman, design: Taddey & Karlin Design *right* Mark Samu, architect: Robert Storm AIA **page 171:** MrSteam **page 173:** *all* Broan-NuTone **page 174:** Mark Lohman, design: Harte Brownlee & Assoc. **page 175:** York Wallcoverings **pages 176–177:** Kichler Lighting **page 178:** *left* Emser Tile *right* melabee m miller, design: Nancee Brown, ASID **page 179:** Mark Lohman, design: Malibu Interiors & Design **page 180:** *top* Plural Design Studio, photography and styling: Mallory Lunke, contractor: Lind Nelson Construction *bottom* York Wallcoverings **page 181:** *left* Mark Samu, design/build: Bonacio Construction *top right* Mark Samu, design: Evergreen Interiors *bottom right* Mary Patton Design, photography: Molly Culver **pages 182–183:** *middle* Eric Roth, design: traskdevelopment.com *top* Olson Photographic, LLC, design/build: Ricci Construction *bottom* Mel Bean Interiors, photography: Laurey Glenn **pages 184–185:** *all* Mary Patton Design, photography: Molly Culver **pages 186–187:** *left* Kichler Lighting *middle* Mel Bean Interiors, photography: Laurey Glenn *right* Dekton by Cosentino **pages 188–189:** *all* Mel Bean Interiors, photography: Kacey Gilpin **page 190:** *left* Eric Roth, design/architect: Hickox Williams *right* Eric Roth, design: Elisa Allen Interiors **page 191:** MrSteam **pages 192–193:** *all* Mark Lohman **pages 194–195:** *middle* Dekton by Cosetino *top right* davidduncanlivingston.com *bottom right* Emser Tile **pages 196–197:** *all* Mark Lohman, architect: Michael Lee Architects **pages 198–199:** *all* davidduncanlivingston.com **pages 200–201:** *all* Mel Bean Interiors, photography: Laurey Glenn **page 202:** *left* Tony Giammarino/Giammarino & Dworkin, design: homemasons.com *right* davidduncanlivingston.com **page 203:** *left* Eric Roth, design: GFCDevelopment.com *right* davidduncanlivingston.com **page 209:** Mary Patton Design, photography: Molly Culver **page 223:** Kichler Lighting **Back cover:** *top* Mr Steam *bottom* Broan-NuTone

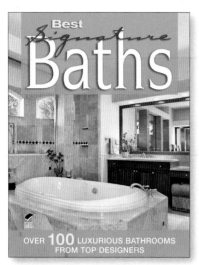
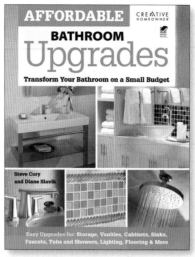

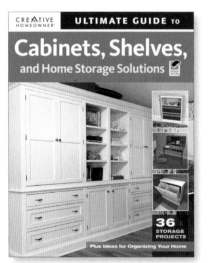
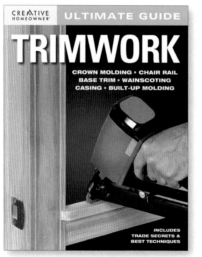
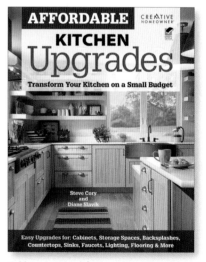